GOLD

GOLD

A TRIPLE CHAMPION'S STORY

MICHELLE SMITH

WITH

CATHAL DERVAN

MAINSTREAM
PUBLISHING

EDINBURGH AND LONDON

For Erik
The wind beneath my wings

First published in 1996 by
MAINSTREAM PUBLISHING COMPANY (EDINBURGH) LTD
7 Albany Street
Edinburgh EH1 3UG

ISBN 1 85158 930 9

A catalogue record for this book is available from the British Library

Typeset in Garamond
Printed and bound in Great Britain by Butler & Tanner Ltd

Contents

Introduction

In the early hours of 21 July 1996, a new question was added to the list of great Irish sporting queries. You know the one: the great debate that invariably starts over a few pints or otherwise in some bar-room and generally develops along the lines of 'Where were you the day JFK was shot?' or 'Where were you the day Elvis Presley died?'

Nowadays in Irish bars, the topic of debate is as likely to cross the sporting divide as it is to enter the world of politics, current affairs or popular entertainment. It's just as likely you'll be asked where you were the day Ronnie Delaney won the gold medal at the Melbourne Olympics in 1956 as to your whereabouts on the day man walked on the moon. If you were alive then of course.

Others may well wonder what you were doing when Mary Peters hit Olympic gold in Mexico; where you were when Ciaran Fitzgerald lifted the Triple Crown for Irish rugby; your position in life when John Treacy won the world cross-country championships in Limerick; where you were when Stephen Roche won the Tour de France; or what you were doing when Ray Houghton scored against England in Stuttgart or against Italy in New Jersey?

They may even ask where you were when Barry McGuigan won the world title against Pedroza; when Steve Collins knocked the stuffing out of Chris Eubank; or when Sonia O'Sullivan lifted gold at the world championships in Gothenburg.

How about your position when Offaly staged their late, late rally to win the 1994 all-Ireland hurling title; when Clare ended their famine a year later; when Jayo and the Dubs triumphed in 1995;

when Wexford ended their hurling quest in 1996.

On that historic Irish morning of Sunday, 21 July 1996, the night before in America, a new question joined the list. 'Where were you when Michelle Smith won gold? When an Irish woman won an Olympic medal for the first time? When Irish swimming celebrated its first Olympic championship victory? When Ireland claimed its first medal of the Atlanta games?'

I wasn't born when Ronnie Delaney hit gold in Australia. I'm too young at 32 to remember where I was when JFK was shot and Oliver Stone didn't include me in the movie. I know I was in a car on the way to a Wicklow holiday when Elvis died.

I can guarantee that I was working in a hayshed in Dunshaughlin, County Meath, when Eamonn Coghlan finished fourth in the 1,500 metres final at the Moscow Olympics. I was in the Gaeil Colmcille GAA centre in Kells when Barry McGuigan finished off Pedroza. I was in the Neckarstadion in Stuttgart when Razor scored against England. I was on hand again when he hit the net against the Italians in the Giants Stadium at the 1994 World Cup finals. I was in a London taxi when Michael Carruth hit the golden trail in his own right in Barcelona four years ago.

All those great moments pale into lesser significance though next to the feats of Michelle Smith at the Atlanta Olympics.

And like the rest of Ireland I know where I was the moment Michelle Smith touched the wall as the first Irish swimmer to win an Olympic event. I know exactly where I was when Irish swimming tasted gold for the first time and enjoyed it: I was in a different time zone, a holiday home in Ownahincha in West Cork when Michelle Smith swam her way into the history books in the early hours of Sunday morning, 21 July 1996. Only the cheers from next door hinted at the greatness unfolding in front of our late-night television eyes. The portable screen did her justice though. A true champion was born in the golden waters of Atlanta. And we cheered her all the way, just as we cheered Houghton and Carruth, O'Sullivan and Collins.

My two young children slept as Michelle swam her way to glory. In years to come I will probably ask them where they were when Michelle Smith won the gold medal. They won't remember only because of their youth.

They will, though, know who Michelle Smith is. For that's the legacy of her victory in the 400 metre individual medley at the

Atlanta games, the legacy of the two golds and one bronze that followed from that first gold from the girl with the golden heart, a girl from a country without a 50-metre pool who won her place in the history of a nation with sporting passion running through its veins.

For that we should all be grateful.

This is Michelle Smith's story. The story of a woman with only one desire in her body – the will to win. The story of a young woman and a boyfriend-turned-coach-turned-husband who helped to make her dream come true.

Gold. The story of an Olympic champion. A triple Olympic champion.

Cathal Dervan,
Dublin, 1996

CHAPTER ONE

A Sort of Homecoming

The route was as familiar as the rain. Out from the city centre and across the Long Mile Road. Follow the signs for the South. Over the new roundabout. Onto the Naas dual carriageway. Pass Newlands Cross; put the foot down outside the Green Isle, and ease onto familiar tracks. The ritual route home from the pool, from the baths of yesteryears in Terenure, Coolmine, King's Hospital, Guinness's, ALSAA. The early mornings and the late nights of formative years.

Later it would become the route home to Rathcoole from foreign waters, from trips abroad. Returns from competition, from 50-metre training sessions, from Olympic camp, from Olympic games, from European Championships, World Cups and World Championships. From trips burdened more with dreams than medals. From trips laden down with golden moments and golden memories.

The route home from England, Scotland, Hong Kong, Vienna, Rome, Seoul, Barcelona, Houston and Holland. Often, from Holland.

This time, though, it was different. This time Michelle Smith was coming home from Atlanta 1996; coming home with the excess baggage of three gold medals and one bronze for dipping her Irish toes in the waters of Georgia.

She was coming home from the Olympic games as a champion, a national hero: the first Irish swimmer to qualify for an Olympic final; the first Irish woman to win an Olympic medal; the first Irish sports star to win four medals in one games. She was the first girl from Dublin to do it in the Olympic world; the first woman to strike gold for Ireland.

Michelle Smith was coming home to Rathcoole, to her parents, to her family and friends, to her own people. This was the homecoming that mattered, the only reception that really mattered. This was an open-topped bus that swept through the rain and into the village of Rathcoole. She was coming home: home to the party, to the hundred thousand welcomes; home to the glorious reality of life as a triple Olympic champion, Ireland's first.

Rathcoole had never looked so good.

CHAPTER TWO

Rathcoole

The swinging sixties: era of the Fab Four, the Rolling Stones, flower power, Volkswagen Beetles and George Best; the decade that saw man walking on the moon and trying to smoke it. But away from Dylan and his own rolling stones, two things happened at the end of the '60s that were to change the face of Irish sporting history; two events occurred that were to alter the course of Irish Olympic endeavour forever.

Firstly, childhood sweethearts Brian Smith and Patricia Traynor, known to one and all as Pat, married on 4 January 1969, at the parish church of Westland Row in Dublin.

Brian and Pat were typical Dubliners, born and reared within walking distance of Clery's clock on O'Connell Street. Brian, the older of the two, was born on Kilworth Road, Drimnagh, in the heart of working-class Dublin. He was an addictive smoker, regularly consuming 50 or 60 of those old-fashioned Woodbines daily until the day he got married; and then he gave them up. Forever.

Sports were a passion for Brian Smith in his formative years but they were not the sports of popular opinion. His passions were hillwalking and tenpin bowling; his membership of the An Oige hostel and youth organisation leading him across Ireland and into the continent.

He started his working life like so many of his peers in the motor industry, working in the great old Ford Corporation that was one of the mainstays of the city's industrial life at that point in time. Brian Smith was never one for rank and file employment though. He wanted to be his own boss, and the year he got married he took another big step. He set up in the spare parts business on his own, first in Newcastle, another Dublin suburb, then in the more populated Clondalkin where, to this day, the name, 'Brian Smith Motor Factors', hangs over the door at Unit 2, Desmond House, Boot Road, Dublin 22.

Pat came from an enclave of Ringsend, beside the old Boland's mill, that was closer to the city centre. She was one of eight children, four girls and four boys, a typical Dublin family in size and nature. They grew up together in Dublin 2 and they stayed together. Life for Pat revolved around her family until the day she met Brian Smith for the second time, on his return from a spell in England. Romance blossomed, and they married.

The newly married Smiths had a traditional Irish wedding, but they did not follow tradition when it came to a choice of family home. Friends and relatives were aghast as the news broke. The Smiths were off to Rathcoole. Some relatives had to ask a second time where it was. Their Dublin didn't stretch the ten miles or so out the Naas Road to the village that was to become home to these true blue Dubs. Rathcoole then was the Wild West as far as your conventional Dubliner was concerned. The sceptics wondered how anyone could choose such a location for their home.

The newly weds had no such problem. They liked the tranquillity their new home offered; they liked the chance to raise a family away from the cut and thrust of life in a city centre. They knew they were moving away from their respective families. They knew they would be grateful in years to come for moving away from the metropolis and to the west.

But first it was to Wexford for the honeymoon, a county that was to play such a large part in the life of the Smith family, a county that was to introduce the eldest of their children to the joys of the water and the wilds. The Smiths honeymooned in Wexford in the year of 1969, a honeymoon marked by their purchase along the way of chairs for their new home and the antics of an old car that was to let them down on their way back home to Dublin.

Rathcoole it was then for Pat and Brian Smith, their chairs from Wexford, a table, a bed and a cooker, enough to start a home and a family in a village far removed from their city-centre roots; a village that offered them a new home at a price of £5 a week at a time when Brian was earning £15. And Rathcoole it has been ever since for the

Smiths and for their children Michelle, Sarah, Aisling and Brian junior.

The second momentous event of that year occurred in December, on the 16th of the month, when a baby girl entered the world, first daughter to the Smiths of Rathcoole, later to become the first lady of Irish swimming and Irish sport. Not surprisingly Michelle Marie Smith was a fighter and a winner from the day she was born ahead of schedule. She wasn't due until the first week of 1970, the first week of a new decade and a new era, a date that would have been far more beneficial later in life when it came to competitive swimming and age group deadlines if she had just waited. Instead, she spent her formative swimming years competing against girls born the same year but anything up to 11 months older, girls with a better physique and a better body strength because of that crucial difference in age.

But Michelle Smith likes doing things the hard way. And on the morning of 16 December 1969 she came screaming into the world in The Coombe hospital, all 7lbs 6oz of her, two weeks ahead of schedule, three weeks before her cousin Alan, son to Aunt Mary and Uncle Gerry was born. The script said he was to be the first of the grandchildren in Pat Smith's mother's house. Nobody told Michelle.

'My Aunt Mary still jokes that I won the first race I ever entered,' remarks Michelle. 'The big battle in the family at the time was to produce the first grandchild for my grandmother. My mother and her sister Mary were both pregnant at the same time, with my aunt due a couple of weeks before I was set to enter this great world of ours. With Christmas coming up, there was great drama in the two households because they both wanted to present the grandchild as the most appropriate seasonal present of all. I won that race when I arrived two weeks ahead of plan – and the ironic thing is that my cousin, Alan, was late. That Christmas, I was the only grandchild, the first, in my mother's family.'

It has been a life of firsts for Michelle Smith and her devoted parents, parents who now deserve to bask in the reflective glory of their daughter's achievements. Brian and Pat Smith have dedicated their lives to their children. It was at their insistence that Michelle Smith first learnt to swim in the baths local to Rathcoole, in the neighbouring Dublin suburbs of Tallaght and Clondalkin. It was their promptings that urged their daughters to take up ballet, Irish dancing, gymnastics and music lessons on alternate Saturday mornings. It was their love for the countryside and fresh air that brought the family to Wexford on family holidays, thereby introducing the Smith girls to the seawater and currents at Curracloe, Hook Head and Rosslare strand. Michelle Smith first fell in love with the water on the campsites of early family holidays. At the age of two, she persistently sat under the tap at the Wexford site, there to feel water running from the pump over her head and down her back.

Michelle takes up the story: 'My parents have always been down-to-earth people with down-to-earth values and ideals. Their life was never elaborate or complicated. They live for their family and they live for each other. Throughout our childhood my parents did whatever had to be done to ensure that we had everything we wanted. They encouraged us to take to sport, to take to the water, to take to the ways of our country and our traditions.

'My father was always adamant that his girls would be involved in some sort of recreation or sport. He never wanted anyone to tell him his kids were hanging around street corners. From an early age they encouraged us to be active and be alive. Irish dancing, music, swimming and ballet were on the agenda, almost as soon as we could walk. It didn't matter what it was, just as long as we were doing something. My father never wanted his children to be classed as corner boys or layabouts. It was bred into us to compete, to be active, and to win.'

The Smiths also had a strong sense of nationality and identity. As a youngster, Brian had been brought through the Christian Brothers educational system. He always had it in mind to ensure that his children grew up with a love for the Irish tongue. And when Michelle Smith's early education didn't go according to plan the seeds were sown to put that particular idea into operation.

'Primary school came for me at five years of age, like all Irish children. My parents sent me first to the local primary school, which is state-funded and state-run. It was the school to go to in Rathcoole, and that first morning I set off without as much as a whimper or even a tear in my eye. That independent spirit was forceful even then. I'm sure my mother was a little upset at the ritual of her eldest child's first day at school, but it didn't bother me, to begin with. Sadly, that happy first taste was not a prelude for what was to come as I became the victim of a school bully.

'I can laugh about it now but it wasn't funny at the time; and I know how traumatic it is for any child living through the nightmare of bullying at school. When the bullying started for me at that first primary school, it was far from a laughing matter. The boy in the desk beside me struck me as a bit different the first day I sat next to him when he took some crayons from his pencil case and began to chew them. Worse followed, when he swallowed the remains of his endeavours. I knew this was no ordinary classmate.

'My worst suspicions were confirmed when he began to pick on me. He'd start fights in the classroom, the playground and after the final bell of the afternoon. When I went home in the evenings, my parents could sense that there was something wrong. When they discovered the cause of my displeasure, they removed me from the national school and enrolled me in the new Scoil Chrónáin, the local Irish-language primary school. There I discovered a language I was to fall in love with, and an educational system that I flourished in. It was one of the best things that ever happened to me.

'Ironically that boy in the desk beside me followed me to the Irish school. Thankfully, he had left his bullying ways behind him. And he's probably living in fear now of the day I'll tell my story to the world. I'll protect his name; but he knows who I'm talking about.'

Michelle Smith – or 'Michelle Nic Gabhann' as she was known in primary school – took to her native language with the same ease with which she was to take to the water. It is a love affair that has blossomed with age; and it was evident during the Olympics in Atlanta when she regularly broke into Irish, speaking with radio broadcaster Sean Ban Breathnach during her gold medal press conferences. She has also promoted the Irish language with *Bord na Gaeilge*, and she has been proud to do so.

People now often ask Michelle why her parents sent her to the Irish school. She tells them: 'With hindsight it was one of the best decisions of their lives and something that I will always be grateful to them for; but at the time, there was no apparent reason. Both my parents had a few words of Irish but they were never fluent in our native tongue, although my father came from a Christian Brothers educational background where the language was a chore rather than a labour of love for the kids. But they wanted us to grow up proud of our language, to feel it was a part of our lives.

'At five years of age it was easy to regard the language as native. At that age, you had no hang-ups, no preconceptions about the Irish tongue. It was as natural as anything to see the word "doras" written on the door, and to know that it meant "door". It was natural to ask permission to go to the toilet in Irish.

'I learnt to love the language. I learnt to be proud of my country, my history, my culture. That is something I will take with me to the grave.

'At secondary level the choice was to go to an English language school in Rathcoole or make the daily journey to Coláiste Chilliain in Clondalkin, an all-Irish school, one of the first second-level schools of its kind in the country. Thankfully, with my parents blessings, I chose the latter.

'I am proud of the fact that I was educated through the medium of the Irish language, and proud of the fact that Irish is one of my primary languages. People ask me now if my education increased my awareness of my nationality. In many ways it did; but like everyone else who has lived abroad, I think my "level" of Irishness increased anyway when I lived first in Houston and then in Holland.

'And ever since the Olympics, more and more people come up to me in the street now and talk to me in Irish. They have seen me promote the language for *Bord na Gaeilge* on the television, and it's great that they take the time out to learn and make the effort to speak in our national language.'

Back in the early '70s, it was rare to see an Irish language primary school in a small Dublin village like Rathcoole. In fact, it was rare to see one outside the Gaeltacht areas, which are primarily in the West, where Irish is, to this day, the first language. The Smiths, Michelle and her sister, Sarah, two years later, were two of the first students in a school that began life without heating, a fact that saw the girls sitting in class with their duffel coats on in those early days.

Michelle recalls, 'The Irish primary school in Rathcoole was one of the first of its kind in the country and one of the most innovative schools of any type. The principal, Brenda McKenna, was one of the most go-ahead people I had ever met. She was keen on the pupils' participation in sports and culture. She organised everything from tin whistle lessons to Irish dancing to swimming in the pool in Tallaght when I was young. And she even set up French lessons as an extra-curricular activity, something that was unheard of for primary students.

'I loved that element of school life. And the trips to the swimming pool were the icing on the cake as far as I was concerned. My dad had encouraged me to swim from an early age, not just because he felt that it would be beneficial from a safety point of view. From the age of five on, he brought me to the pools in Clondalkin and Tallaght and into the sea at Wexford where we'd go for family holidays in the summer.'

Gradually the swimming bug began to bite for Michelle Smith. By the age of nine she was ready for action in the community games, a huge festival of sport that brings children of all ages into competition in every sport imaginable. First the kids compete at local level for the right to represent their county in the national finals at the Mosney Holiday Centre in County Meath.

Then they compete for their county on one of the most prestigious breeding grounds for Irish sport, a platform that has played host to Olympic athletes like Sonia O'Sullivan and soccer players like Niall Quinn, of Sunderland and Ireland, in the past. Michelle Smith was ready for the community games at nine years of age. She won the Dublin leg of the competition, swimming for Rathcoole, but failed to finish amongst the medallists at the national finals in Mosney. Along the way though, she did attract the attentions of a man who was to spot the raw talent that was later to realise Olympic ambition.

'To train for the community games, my dad would drive me up to the pool in Tallaght every Sunday morning. One day when we were there, a man called Jack Mason approached my dad and got talking about my ability and my potential as a swimmer. He mentioned the fact that he was involved with the Terenure College swimming club and asked my dad to bring me along one Sunday morning. That was my first introduction to organised swimming. Up until then we had contented ourselves with the family trips to the pool and the advent of the community games in Rathcoole.

'My dad took Jack up on the offer and straightaway I was enrolled as a member of Terenure under the watchful eye of the coach, Larry Williamson, a man who had coached Irish swimmers at national and Olympic levels and a man whose son, Kevin, had swum for Ireland at the 1980 Olympics in Moscow. Larry was a good coach. He knew what he was doing and, to this day, I still prefer to go up to the pool at Terenure College whenever I want to train while I'm at home.

'However, the one problem with the Terenure club at that point in time was the fact that the majority of the members were older, ranging in age from 16 or 17 upwards. At nine, I was in the minority; I was out on a limb, training in a side lane while the senior swimmers were pushed to the limits by Larry. In some ways, that may have been a good thing. It pushed me because I was constantly trying to keep up with people who were much older than I was. That also explains why I only spent two years with the Terenure club: I needed kids my own age, swimmers at my own level. So I moved slightly closer to home – to the King's Hospital club in Palmerstown, on the main Dublin–Galway road. That was more like my natural swimming home, but I will never forget what Larry and the Terenure club did for me in my earliest swimming years. They knew I only left because I needed more kids my own age around me.

'Just after I left Terenure for the King's Hospital club, I got the trip of a lifetime to Hong Kong in 1980. I was the last-minute replacement for one of the more senior girls who had to pull out of the trip. It was a fantastic experience to go off to the Far East at 11 years of age and compete in a 50-metre pool. But what was more memorable about the place was the buzz that only a city in the Far East can boast: the fish shops down on the quayside and the busy harbour. I will never forget the harbour. We were brought out there as VIP guests on this incredible yacht. It was an experience.'

It was the first amazing experience of an amazing relationship between swimming and swimmer. Michelle Smith would return to Hong Kong in January 1995 and claim two gold medals in a World Cup meeting to signal her arrival on the international stage.

CHAPTER THREE

Palmerstown

Larry Williamson was one of the great influences on Michelle Smith in her early years as a swimmer. He saw a raw talent that was there to be developed the first day Jack Mason brought her to the swimming club attached to Terenure College on Dublin's southside. Sadly, Larry was not there to witness her greatest triumphs. He died a year after Michelle Smith had left Terenure for the King's Hospital club.

Her move was destined. The club's Palmerstown base was 25 minutes' drive from the Smith family home in Rathcoole. The fact that another girl, Shayne Gordon from the nearby Saggart, joined the King's Hospital club at the same time, helped make the transition all the easier for Michelle. And there were more people Michelle's age involved, something that had always been a problem at Terenure where Michelle trained with the adults or on her own.

In Palmerstown she found a new home for her swimming dream, spiritually and literally. This was better. She felt more at ease. And she came under the watchful eye of coaches Sandra Elders, firstly, and then Derry O'Rourke. Incredibly, O'Rourke at first saw little in the new girl to believe she would make it as a swimmer. Before he ever knew the size of Michelle Smith's heart he had dismissed her on the basis of her small physical stature. He told her father so. Told Brian Smith his daughter would never make it in the pool. Years later Derry O'Rourke was to cringe at the memory of that rather speedy judgement.

Like all Irish swimming clubs King's Hospital was left to fend for itself. The sport of swimming in Ireland is funded in part by Irish government grants, but only in a very small part. The lack of a 50-

metre pool shocks visitors and competitors from abroad. It is merely symptomatic of a national problem where sport is left to look after itself until glory commands the attention – and subsequently the money of the politicians. Swimming clubs therefore exist in pools that are mainly funded by public swimming times. Pool time for the clubs is generally available only very early in the morning. This explains why the Smith household woke every morning for six mornings a week to the sound of their eldest daughter and the accompaniment of her swimming dream. A dream that was to prosper in the formative years of her sporting career at King's Hospital as she grew in strength and stature.

Eventually familiarity bred contentment for club coach O'Rourke. He studied Michelle's stroke in the Palmerstown pool and decided that Williamson had been right. There was real talent in the new girl, talent that could lead to success on the international stage. She looked comfortable and confident in the water. There was strength in her arms, power in her shoulders, rhythm in her stroke. More than anyone else in the Palmerstown club this new girl looked a swimmer – a natural born swimmer.

When Michelle was only 12 years of age, the King's Hospital coach made a bold prediction. Michelle Smith was good enough to go to the Olympics, good enough to train for the 1988 games, six years later, in the Korean city of Seoul. It was a brave prediction from a man who was to go on to coach the Irish international squad. A prediction that delighted Michelle Smith and her family. A prediction that should have triggered panic and pride in equal measure. A prediction that could have ruined her swimming career if she had taken it too seriously.

'Looking back now,' Michelle says, 'it was a crazy age to tell any child that they could make it to an Olympic games. At 12 years of age you are too young, too impressionable not to believe it. For me the Olympics had always been something special. My father had been a keen follower of the Olympic games. He encouraged us to watch it with him, to marvel at the exploits of the great athletes like Coe and Ovett in the '80s. To be told at 12 years of age that I could follow them onto the Olympic stage in Seoul six years later was only filling my head with dreams. In hindsight that was dangerous.'

Dangerous as it may have been it did not stop an incredibly competitive streak developing in the eldest of the Smith girls. An international career was in its infancy. Prompted by O'Rourke's predictions, Smith took her swimming seriously. At the age of 12 she was training 20 hours a week, up and down the pool, following instructions often left on the blackboard by coaches with neither the time nor the resources to concentrate on individual needs. In hindsight, Michelle sees the dangers of strenuous training at that early age. Back then it was accepted as part of the route to Seoul. And, in fairness, it worked in the circumstances. By the age of 13, Michelle Smith was good enough not just to win the Dublin Community Games but also the national finals in Mosney.

It didn't stop there either, as she made her mark in national junior competition. By the age of 14, Michelle was good enough to pip Aisling McElwee to numerous Irish titles and represent her country in a major multi-national championships in Europe. On the home front she had her most successful season ever when she won a record 13 medals, 11 gold and two silver, at the National Championships in Bangor, Co. Down. Seoul was looking good. The prospects then improved when she became the first Irish swimmer to dip below five minutes for the 400-metre individual medley short course, a championship she did not lose between 1984 and 1995.

All that was the result of hard work and dedication. Michelle Smith was dedicated to her sport. Her father was dedicated to his daughter and her burning ambition to prove Larry Williamson and Derry O'Rourke right.

Something had to give. Michelle Smith trained in the morning, went to school, often trained again in the evenings then went home to study for school the next day. She found it hard going in the classroom, her head occasionally dropping to the desk in sheer exhaustion. Thankfully, the staff and pupils at Coláiste Chilliain were sympathetic to her needs. Teachers held material back for her when she was away on training courses or in competition. Pupils kept an eye out for the star in the making, helping her with classes she had missed, making it easier for her to concentrate on her swimming when it really mattered.

Her father rose early every morning to bring her to the pool, catching up on his sleep in the back of his van as Michelle trained for two hours at the King's Hospital. That became a ritual in the household. Brian Smith was also conscious of the need to be fair to his daughter. He was proud of his daughter's prowess in the pool, proud of her ability as she swam her way up through the Irish rankings. He was also aware of his duties as a parent to such a gifted child. Michelle Smith's father wanted to ensure that it was her ambition and not his that had her in a pool at a time when others were turning over for their second sleep. He wanted to test the water so to speak, to see how much she really wanted to swim, how much she herself wanted to succeed. He got his chance, almost by accident.

One morning he found it particularly difficult to raise his daughter from her exhausted slumbers after a 5.15 alarm call. Brian Smith decided to take action. If Michelle wanted it badly enough she would have to ensure the pair of them were up sufficiently early to make her early morning pool time in Palmerstown. That night he gave Michelle the alarm clock. If she wanted to be up in time, she could take charge of the timekeeping. Then he would know if it was his hunger or hers that drove them out of the door every morning, winter, spring or fall.

Michelle now says, 'In many ways my dad was testing me with the alarm clock that morning. He was worried that my ambition was being stifled by his pride in his daughter, by his desire to see me succeed. He needed proof that I wanted to win. He wanted to see if I had the desire to make it in the pool, to see if I was hungry enough to get up every morning before the crack of dawn, get him up and get to the training session.

'I never missed one alarm clock call from that day on but I have to admit now that it was hard. I was a bit young to do that much. Nowadays coaches are a lot more cautious about overtraining children. If you start heavy training at ten then by the time you are 20 you may get sick of it.'

Away from the pool Michelle was marked as an academic of the future by the teachers at Coláiste Chilliain in Clondalkin. Her time was devoted more to swimming than study but still the girl was a natural when it came to education. The intermediate certificate examinations produced a flood of honours results. She was a gifted student and she came through subjects with flying colours. Her parents sat her down and talked her through her future. Her future was swimming. Her future was communications. Even at that young age she had an eye on the world of communication, an interest and a qualification that was to serve so well in the years to come.

In the pool at King's Hospital, the young Michelle Smith was to develop as the major arrival in the world of Irish women's swimming. She was to take the national limelight and national titles away from her peer McElwee. Michelle was also to develop an intriguing battle with Aileen Convery, the Glenalbyn girl who was to accompany Smith to the 1988 Olympics in Seoul. At club level she was to come under the wing of Catherine Bohan, Olympian in 1980 and a highly experienced star of the senior circuit who was to do her bit to develop the young Michelle Smith. Bohan had travelled the world. She had gone to America on a sports scholarship to Iowa University. She knew the pain and the effort it took to become an Olympic-class swimmer. She was more than willing to share information with the young girl from Rathcoole, more than willing to pass on her experience – warts and all.

If Michelle Smith wanted to make it she now knew how tough it was. A girl who had once tormented holidaymakers on a caravan site in Wexford by sitting under the only water tap with a constant drip descending on her head was in love with swimming. She wanted to succeed. She had the desire and the hunger. At 14 she was getting there. By 15 she was on the way.

Michelle recalls: 'I had a great year at 14 as I began to develop at King's Hospital from the help that Catherine was giving me. That year I won national senior and junior titles and I also made the Irish team for the European junior championships in Luxembourg. That in itself was a major step forward. I didn't win a medal but I did compete at international level. That meant a lot, both to me and to my family. The other kids at school in Clondalkin stopped wondering about this crazy sport I was into. They stopped wondering why anybody would get up at 5.15 in the morning to get the benefit of pool time. They stopped asking why I spent the first two hours of my day going up and down a swimming pool in Palmerstown. They could see I was making progress and they were happy for me.'

They weren't the only ones. National coach George Gibney had Michelle on his six-strong team of élite swimmers training and competing for the Seoul Olympics. They were the chosen few, monitored by the national coaches, nurtured for greatness.

When Michelle Smith made the qualifying time for the 1985 European senior championships, O'Rourke and Gibney knew their inclinations had been confirmed. This girl was good. Very good.

CHAPTER FOUR

Seoul

Michelle Smith was told that she could swim at the Seoul Olympics when she was only 12. When she was 18, she went to the 1988 Olympics in the Far East – but it was not without a lot of blood, sweat and tears. In 1985 she had made the qualifying time for the 200-metre backstroke at the European Championships. The following year her aim was to qualify for the World Championships in Madrid, the last big world test before the Olympic games in the Far East.

Michelle needed a time of 2:19.50 to make the world finals. She never got there. At the National Championships she was bang on target, bang on the qualifying time. The IASA though decided not to send Michelle to those Championships in Spain. They decided her qualification time had been too late to justify her inclusion in the Irish team; it was close, but not close enough.

It was all beginning to get to the girl from Rathcoole. She wanted to compete at the highest level. She was afraid that she was never going to get there without taking action. At just 17 years of age that's exactly what Michelle Smith did. She took the course of her career into her own hands.

First, she put her education on hold for a year. She took a sabbatical from Coláiste Chilliain for 12 months and put her leaving certificate examinations, her final exams in secondary school, back a year. Education could wait. Her swimming ambitions couldn't.

She began training full time, but she was not happy with the format. The national coach, George Gibney, was also associated with the Trojan club. Michelle felt almost isolated at the King's Hospital.

She was tired of the old routines, the same training schedules. She wanted a new challenge, a new method to bring her up to the international standard she craved.

In late 1987, Michelle Smith took off for Canada, for a swimming club in Calgary run by the respected Canadian coach, Deryk Snelling. For 20 years he had been one of the most respected coaches on the North American continent. He had produced a dozen world-class swimmers for Canada. He had sent swimmers to Olympic games and World Championships – and he welcomed them back with medals in their pockets. He now presented Michelle Smith with the challenge her career had been waiting for.

Michelle took up the challenge. 'I knew I needed to do something. For five years I had been building up towards the Olympics. Now I needed to step up a class in both competition and training to justify that status. Canada was an option made available to me through the King's Hospital club. It was a big step to take, but when I had weighed up all the pros and cons and discussed it with my parents, it was the right thing to do. Derry O'Rourke from King's Hospital knew Deryk Snelling and respected him as a top-class coach.

'The benefit of training in a 50-metre pool was also a huge advantage. My experience at the 50-metre pool standard had been limited to competition in Europe. I needed long-distance training before the Olympics. Calgary gave me all that and more. It introduced me to another culture, to a way of life that I could quite easily have settled into, that I almost settled into before the Olympics in Barcelona four years later.

'It also gave me a glimpse of what was needed to succeed as a top-class swimmer. It was the first time I had really been exposed to the work and dedication that was needed to make it onto the winners' podium. In Calgary, I was surrounded by top-class swimmers. There were a dozen Canadian Olympic hopefuls working with Deryk Snelling. The set-up and the attitude to training were professional in every way.

'We lived to swim. The morning and evening sessions in the pool were so different to anything I had experienced at home. Deryk and his coaches worked out a programme to build me up for Seoul. They built up my fitness. They sent me out running to develop my stamina. They showed me how to work to compete and I relished it. I wanted more.

'Even the swimmers I trained with taught me things. Their goals were so much higher than mine. They were going to Seoul to win. I was going there to compete. There was a subtle difference and they showed it to me in Canada.

'A good percentage of them made it to the Olympics. One of them, Mark Tewksbury, went on to win the gold medal in the 100-metre backstroke at the Barcelona games in 1992. I raced with the team in the Canadian Championships and we won medals. That was a big indictment for my decision to go out there. The training was paying off. I was feeling good. After three months in Canada living for my sport I went home to Ireland a better swimmer and a better fighter. The hunger was there at last.'

Michelle Smith went home to discover that her place on the Olympic team was guaranteed. The Olympic Council of Ireland had decided to send a team of four swimmers to the Seoul games. For the first time, real money was being made available to Irish swimming. Michelle Smith and the other members of the team, Gary O'Toole, Aileen Convery and Stephen Cullen, received figures in the region of £1,000 to £1,500 each to subsidise their training. The fifth person, Omagh man Richard Gheel, was to make a late charge for a qualifying time and was belatedly added to the squad. More importantly, the national coach George Gibney was given the money he needed to bring the team abroad for long-course training in the build-up to Seoul.

Popular opinion had it that this was the best Irish swimming squad ever. Or so they said in the days leading up to a games that will always be remembered for the Ben Johnson drugs scandal. It was the best funded, the best prepared, the most highly motivated squad ever sent out to competition under an Irish flag. If ever an Irish team was going to make the breakthrough, this was it; as the lack of a 50-metre pool at home saw them training over the longer courses in Hawaii, Florida, Britain and France.

The party of five held 12 national records between them as they flew from Dublin to Hawaii for last-minute 50-metre pool work, and then on to Seoul for the '88 Olympics. Bray resident O'Toole, of the Trojan club, was the best known of them all. He was the UCD student then touted as the rising star of Irish swimming. He was expected to break national records in the 100-metre and 200-metre breaststroke and the 200-metre individual medley. At one stage, in

1988, O'Toole was ranked ninth in the world in the breaststroke ratings. He was joined in the men's team by Cullen from Raheny and Gheel from Omagh.

Michelle Smith and Glenalbyn's US-based college student, Aileen Convery, flew the flag for Mna na hEireann. Their backstroke rivalry was carried into the 100-metre and 200-metre events in Korea, with Michelle also entered in the 200-metre and 400-metre individual medleys. Michelle felt good going to Seoul. At one point that year, she was ranked 19th in the world in the 200-metre backstroke, a reward for her months of training in Canada.

In truth, Michelle Smith did not go to Seoul to win medals. This was not her time. It was a chance to experience the Olympic dream, to compete in the same games that had captivated her as a child as she sat with her father in their Rathcoole home and watched the great moments of Montreal, Moscow and Los Angeles. It was a chance to prepare for the glories to come, in years to come.

The Seoul Olympics began for Michelle Smith on Sunday, 18 September 1988, when she posted a personal best and a new Irish long-course record of 5:01.84 in the heats of the 400-metre individual medley. Michelle finished second to Japan's Hiroyo Haraua but ended up 17th overall, just 0.1 of a second outside the 'B' final requirement. Haraua only pulled clear in the final stages of the race. It was heartbreaking for Michelle, who knew she had been so close to a 'B' final, so close to a real breakthrough at world level.

Her next event was the 100-metre backstroke the following Thursday, a less likely event for the King's Hospital girl who had won a silver medal over the distance at an eight-nation contest in Edinburgh the previous July, but whose forte was distance racing and not sprints. The two Irish girls were drawn together in heat three of the 100-metre backstroke. Michelle Smith won her own personal duel when she was just outside Aileen Convery's Irish record in a personal best time of 1:06.22 to finish third in the heat with her close rival in fifth place. Bolin Wang of China took the honours in the heat with Japan's Tomoko Onogi ahead of Michelle in second. Those times left Michelle Smith 27th and Aileen Convery 29th out of 41 starters. By Irish domestic standards, they were good times. They were shown up though in heat five of the qualifiers when the great East German swimmer, Cornelia Sirch, won in a time of 1:01.63.

It didn't get any better for Michelle in the heats for the 200-metre individual medley when she finished fifth behind the Australian, Donna Roctor, in a time of 2:25.53. And in her final event, the 200-metre backstroke, Michelle Smith finished 17th, with Aileen Convery 18th of a field of 34. Still, Michelle had seen a glimpse of what was needed for Olympic glory when she finished seventh in her heat to the East German, Cornelia Sirch.

Michelle says: 'The biggest regret – the only regret – I have from Seoul is the 400-metre individual medley. Now it doesn't seem a big deal to qualify for a "B" final; but back then that would have been seen as a real breakthrough. I was so close and yet so far in the heat. That was the soul-destroying part of it. But aside from that disappointment, I enjoyed every minute of Seoul: the atmosphere in the village; the excitement of a Far Eastern city; the exposure to a culture that was so different from our own. If only the swimming had been that little bit better.'

A year later, Michelle Smith took her leaving certificate examination through Irish and passed with honours in all seven subjects. Irish swimming also made a breakthrough in the year of 1989. Michelle Smith was one member of the Irish team that went to Bonn for the European Championships. Another, Gary O'Toole, won a silver medal in the 200-metre breaststroke.

Michelle remembers: 'There was such a feeling of pride at the poolside when they raised the Irish flag in Gary's honour at the medal ceremony that day. The Irish team had gone to Bonn with nobody giving us a chance of winning anything. Gary surprised them all. He turned in the race of his life to win the silver medal. He had finally put Irish swimming on the map. That was such a proud day.'

Many more proud days were to follow for Irish swimming – and for Michelle Smith. The work started by Gary O'Toole in Germany was to be carried on by Michelle Smith in Rome, in Vienna and in Atlanta. But first, there was the matter of a swimming scholarship to America.

CHAPTER FIVE

Barcelona

The summer of 1989 was the summer of opportunity for Michelle Smith. Armed with an all-honours leaving certificate and a Seoul Olympic stamp of approval, she was the Irish swimmer the American colleges all wanted. America was the next logical step in her swimming education. Collegiate competition and training have always been recognised as a step forward for an aspiring competitor. Her good friend, Catherine Bohan, had come through it the better for the experience.

Four colleges made scholarship offers with Michelle's fees and living expenses paid for. She plumped for Houston, Texas, and a communications degree course that would leave her qualified for a job in the media. The presence at the Texas college of veteran American coach Phill Hansell had swung the decision in Houston's favour. He had been highly rated as a coach worldwide for over 40 years.

It was a mistake. Hansell's training methods were as old as his age. Smith, enlightened by her time in Canada with Deryk Snelling, was hungry for revolution on the coaching front. She was sick and tired of the old ways, of swimming lengths. The repetition of that familiar routine bored her. The Irish girl and the American coach clashed. He knew that she was strong willed and had her own opinions – a fact which he shared with the American public when he was interviewed at the Atlanta games. The coach and the star swimmer agreed to disagree.

The competitive end of things was fine though: swimming in the NCAA Championships, travelling across southern America, and

31

sampling everything from 25-yard to 50-metre pools, all of which helped to mould the competitive animal that Michelle Smith is today. The coaching remained a major disappointment though. Michelle wondered if Canada would have been a better bet, if one of the other colleges would have been a better choice. She wondered if she would ever find a coach to match her needs.

The American university itself was fine – in the classroom. Suffice to say that Michelle never got the education in the pool she had hoped for. Still, away from the pool, Michelle was ill at ease with some aspects of life at Houston University. Some remnants of racism were alive and well, and living in Texas. When she spoke to black friends, fellow sportsmen and sportswomen, she was sometimes scorned by her white colleagues. That was a shock to the system; it left a bad taste in Michelle Smith's mouth. She found some Americans at college hard to stomach. Their racist ways were not her ways.

Her best friend was the Filipino swimmer, Christine Bautistsa, who is, significantly, still a close friend today. They hung out together, regularly visiting the Irish bar, Kenneally's, and changing the rules of darts. They needed something to break the monotony of American life.

Michelle commented: 'With hindsight, it would be easy to say that Houston was a mistake. Eventually Phill and I agreed to disagree on coaching. He was too old-fashioned in his views for my liking. He had put many swimmers onto international teams so that he wasn't going to change his ways for a young girl from Ireland. In the end, I just had to accept that and get on with it.

'The racist thing was just unacceptable! I had thought America had left all that behind when I took up the offer from Houston. Instead, it was alive and kicking in some people in Texas. That was hard to accept.'

A year before the Barcelona Olympics, Michelle Smith went back to Calgary in Canada to train with Deryk Snelling. It was only then that she realised just how wrong the American way had been for her. A bronze medal in the 200-metre backstroke at the Canadian Championships after a couple of weeks of training with Snelling confirmed it. After Barcelona, things would have to change. They did; but in a way she could never have envisaged.

After sending a five-strong team to Seoul four years earlier, the Irish squad was down to just two for the Barcelona games, Michelle

Smith and Gary O'Toole. In truth, Michelle should never have competed at the Barcelona Olympics. And she may never have met her husband.

During April/May, the Irish team went to Arizona for altitude training and competed at an invitational meet in Florida that included the top American swimmers, amongst them Janet Evans.

Michelle was due to swim against Evans at that Olympic training camp. She never made the race. As she dived in for a warm-up swim, Michelle felt something go in her back. For a matter of seconds, she was paralysed. The Irish coach, Derry O'Rourke, realised at the far end of the pool that something had gone badly wrong with his star. O'Rourke and the team physiotherapist lifted Michelle from the pool. She spent the rest of the competition in agony, unable to swim, receiving constant treatment on the back injury that should have ended her Olympic dream there and then.

It didn't. Examination of the injured back when she returned home failed to highlight the sprained disc. Michelle began to live and train with the pain. She was advised that all would be well with the injury by the time the games came around. She took that advice. It was wrong.

Politically, all was not well in the Irish camp before the games that were to produce a gold medal for Michael Carruth and a silver for Belfast's Wayne McCullough. A major row had erupted when the Olympic Council of Ireland had refused to ratify the recommendation of the Irish Amateur Swimming Association giving permission for Marion Madine and Gina Galligan to join Gary O'Toole and Michelle Smith in Barcelona. But Michelle had little time to worry about the politics of Irish sport. She was still concerned about that pain in her back which refused to go away.

Before that injury, Michelle Smith had had no intention of going to Barcelona just to make up the numbers. She had finished 12th in the 400-metre individual medley at the World Championships in Australia the previous year. She was ranked 16th in the world for the same distance over the short course, and had set a new national and all-comers record for the distance of 4:49.58 at the Euromeet in Dublin the previous November. So, it was a realistic aim to look for a place in the final of the 400-metre individual medley, had everything been right in Barcelona. Michelle says: 'I was confident all year that I could take a chunk out of my best time for the event, a time that had seen me 12th in the world the previous year when I had finished fourth in the "B" final at the World Championships in Perth; although, in the year before Barcelona, while I was studying at Houston, I had cut four seconds off my best time in the short course but had not really been trying any long-course competition.'

That Perth swim should have been a warning to some of the familiar names. 'In Australia, I had been leading in my heat at the halfway mark, ahead of the Seoul champion, Janet Evans, and one or two other good swimmers. That told me that I had the ability to succeed against anybody, but it had happened only after the butterfly and backstroke legs which were my strongest at the time. Then it all got away from me on the breaststroke; but it helped me to recognise that I would get nowhere unless I improved in that aspect of the race. That's what I had really worked on before the injury and it was paying off. I proved that at the World Championships in Australia.

'Nobody laughed at Irish swimming after Perth. The swimming world knew now what Gary and I were capable of prior to the '92 Olympics. The days of blaming things on the lack of a 50-metre pool were gone.'

Honour did come Michelle Smith's way in Barcelona when she was selected to carry the Irish flag into the Montjuic Stadium arena at the opening ceremony for the 25th Olympiad, an honour that had been bestowed on her good friend, Wayne McCullough, four years earlier in Seoul. Michelle had missed the Korean opening ceremony because she had to be in the pool the next morning. The same sequence of events befell her in Spain – but she never once entertained the idea of refusing to carry her national flag.

Now, the OCI president, Pat Hickey, who had made his peace with the swimming people after refusing to ratify the selection of Gina Galligan and Marion Madine for the games, nominated Michelle Smith as the first Irish woman to carry the flag.

Michelle says, 'It was a great honour. There was never any thought in my mind that I would turn it down, even with the race the next day. I had expected to skip the ceremony altogether, and to watch it on television back in the Olympic village. But discreet plans were made for me to carry the flag into the stadium for the parade, and then to slip out of the back door and back into bed before anyone could even notice that I was missing. It didn't work, however, and I was in the stadium for hours!'

Michelle's fluency in her native tongue also came in handy when she answered an SOS from Radio na Gaeltachta's Michel O'Se for an interview *as gaeilge*. That was to become a regular feature of the Barcelona games on the Irish language station.

Michelle went into the heats for the 400-metre individual medley at the Picornell pool high above Barcelona knowing that the odds were stacked heavily against her. Her worst fears were realised when she finished 26th out of the 32 women engaged. And her time was of scant consolation: a disappointing 4:58.94 which had left her third in her heat, but more than 2.5 seconds short of her national record, and a full 16 seconds short of the fastest qualifier, Krisztina Egerszeggi of Hungary, who then went on to win the gold medal again.

Michelle recalls: 'There was a hint of hope at the end of the opening butterfly leg, but the backstroke let me down, even when I had got up to second.

'In my other swims, the splits were right for me to break the Irish record, but I think I was trying too hard on what was my favourite discipline. I had had two good backstroke swims in practice; but when the big moment came, my stroke was so choppy that I simply could not pull water. I had tried too hard, and it never flowed. It had not been the type of start I had wanted; but I had enough confidence in my own ability to believe that I still could produce a couple of big performances before the championship was over.'

Michelle Smith trailed in third behind the New Zealander Phillippa Langrell and the South African Jeannine Steenkamp. Neither Langrell nor Steenkamp made the final which Egerszeggi won ahead of China's Lin Li, with Summer Sanders of the United States third.

Things did not get any better when Michelle Smith returned to the pool for the 200-metre individual medley the following Thursday. Again, she failed to produce her best form, struggling throughout the heat, and was relegated to 32nd place in an entry of 37. Her time of 2:23.83 was more than a second outside her career best. Michelle had started in her heat comfortably enough, and she had led after the butterfly leg; unfortunately, she was overtaken by the heat winner, Jill Bruckman of South Africa, and ended in fourth place after a disappointing freestyle leg in the final 50 metres.

The final day of the gala brought nothing but the same old story for Michelle Smith and Gary O'Toole, who was suffering just as much in the Spanish sun. Michelle delivered poorly in the 200-metre backstroke heats, 3.5 seconds off her personal best in a time of 2:21.37 to finish fourth in her heat and 35th overall. Gi Thomson of the Philippines won the heat ahead of Li Lin, the world record breaker in the 200-metre individual medley final. But they both failed to make the top eight as Egerszeggi added the 200-metre backstroke crown to the 400-metre one she had won on the opening day.

So Barcelona was written off as a bad experience by Michelle Smith. She questioned her future in swimming; and she questioned her desire to train hard for another four years before Atlanta. She wondered if she would ever realise the potential flowing through her veins. Then she met a Dutch thrower. The rest, as they say, is history.

CHAPTER SIX

Erik

Barcelona was to change Michelle Smith's life. Her pre-Olympic injury and the subsequent disappointment in the pool made her question her future involvement in the sport that had dominated her life for 13 years. Then came a chance meeting in a Catalonian canteen at the heart of the Olympic village. Love was on her schedule for the first time.

Boyfriends had never been high on the agenda for the girl with the long strawberry-blonde hair from the village of Rathcoole. She was too busy to think about romance; too busy training in the pool, studying at school and working towards that Olympic dream. There had been a brief flirtation with one boy, another swimmer, but Michelle had neither the inclination nor the time to work on their relationship and it never made it past the getting-to-know-you stage. Her family was not surprised.

Michelle was not one to bring boys home to mammy and daddy. 'Her sister, Sarah, made up for her,' they regularly laughed, in the cosiness of family familiarity. 'It was a home with a path beaten to the front door by young fellows chasing after Sarah.' Michelle was not in the same league; she wasn't interested. Swimming was all that mattered.

After her disappointments in the Catalonian waters in 1992, Michelle Smith immersed herself in the spirit of the Olympics. Her good friends, Michael Carruth and Wayne McCullough, were flying their Dublin and Belfast flags in the boxing ring. She felt proud of them, almost a part of them, part of their glory as they fought their way to gold and silver medals respectively. She cheered with the rest of the Irish team now consigned to the role of Olympic spectators after the end of their respective involvement. When Irish team-mate Perri Williams, a race walker, suggested that Michelle join her and her Dutch boyfriend, Harold Van Beek, for lunch and a coffee in the Olympic canteen it was easy to say, 'Yes'. 'Yes'; the most important 'yes' of her young life. Perri's boyfriend had brought a Dutch athlete along with him for company that hot and humid Spanish lunch-time. He was a Dutch discus thrower by the name of Erik de Bruin.

In 1992, Erik de Bruin was aged 29, a world-class discus thrower who had collected the silver medal at the 1991 World Championships in Tokyo. Throwing was in his blood. His mother, Anneke, had been Dutch champion seven times. His sister, Corrie, is still a member of the Dutch Olympic squad.

Erik de Bruin had pulled out of the Barcelona Olympics a month before competition began, the rigours of glandular fever eventually persuading him that his body was not ready for Olympic competition. Instead he went to Spain as a coach to the Dutch team and decathlete Robert de Wit, and ended up in the company of one of the Dutch walkers as he went to meet his Irish girlfriend for a lunch-time coffee. That Irish girlfriend brought Michelle Smith along. The rest is almost history.

'I had never really been involved with any boy before,' says Michelle. 'I think if I had brought a boyfriend home to my parents' house while I was still living at home, my mother would have died of fright. This was different though. When I looked at Erik that day, I saw a handsome, intelligent, charming, humorous man, a man I could identify with, a man I could feel comfortable with. He was both interested and interesting. We talked; we laughed; we felt comfortable in each other's company. He was good to be around, good to be with, good to be seen with. I liked him. When lunch broke up, I had a choice: to risk never seeing him again or to put my head on the block. I opted for the latter course of action, put my heart on my sleeve and asked him if he fancied doing something that night.'

Erik agreed straightaway. 'I liked this girl from Ireland the first time I met her that lunch-time . . .'

The pair went back to their respective national blocks and sought more information on the Olympic information channel that was available on computer to all the athletes. Erik learnt enough about Michelle to be interested. Michelle learnt enough about Erik to be even more interested. Their first date was over dinner and a stroll through the heart of the *Ramblas* in tourist Barcelona. For the rest of the final Olympic week, they were virtually inseparable. Cupid had struck gold.

When the time came to leave Barcelona and the Olympics, Michelle Smith and Erik de Bruin exchanged kisses and swapped phone numbers. He went back to Holland, and she went home to Ireland. They phoned; they talked; she invited him over to Dublin for a holiday. He agreed and arrived on the ferry in Dun Laoghaire in his Dutch Olympic team car to be greeted by the entire Smith family. If Michelle was bringing a boy home, then it was well worth a look.

Michelle's father, Brian, remembers it well. 'We liked him the first minute we met him. A big, tall, good-looking young fellow. He knew nothing about swimming but we liked him.'

Erik de Bruin and Michelle Smith spent ten days together that autumn touring Ireland. She introduced him to Irish ways and Irish laws, the rugged coastline of the West, and the waters of Wexford where she had first tasted the salt of the sea and developed the desire to swim. He liked the country – and he liked his guide. They grew closer, too close to part until necessity stepped in. And when Erik went back to Holland and Michelle returned to university in America, they knew their parting was destined not to last.

He rang the States persistently that autumn and into the winter. She felt the strings of her heart tugging. She was coming home. He agreed to move to Ireland. That Christmas she took a flight out of Houston and they were briefly reunited in Erik's native Holland; then they threw a few things into his car and took off on the boat to Ireland. They were going home to Michelle's native city to start a new life – together. They landed on the doorstep at the Smith family home in Rathcoole and moved in. They have hardly been apart since; almost never.

Two days before Christmas, the Dutch thrower and the Irish swimmer took a seasonal stroll down Dublin's Grafton Street. In all the fuss surrounding the move to Ireland, Erik had forgotten to buy Michelle a Christmas present. He stopped her outside Weirs Jewellers and asked her if she liked any of the engagement rings. Michelle picked one out, he bought it, and a marriage made in heaven was underway.

Michelle takes up the story: 'It just seemed the most natural thing in the world to do right then. I knew he was right for me and vice versa. It has been that way for all the time we have known each other. This was the real thing.

'A lot of things about him attracted me from the word "go", and made me realise that he was right for me. I liked his sense of humour. We just seemed to get along very well right from the beginning and it seemed natural for our relationship to develop so quickly. When he left after our first holiday around Ireland, I had a fair idea that he was special. I don't know how to explain it but I knew in my heart and soul that he was the one for me. I went back to America but to be fair, university never stood a chance. Something deep inside wanted me to go home, to be with Erik, to be together as a couple. He had started to ask questions about my swimming, about my coaching, about my ambition. I knew he could help me. I knew we should be together. That winter I opted out of my university course, flew to Holland and then Erik and I moved to Ireland. Until that time, I had never even mentioned a boy's name in my parents' company; but I rang them from America to tell them I was coming home to live with my Dutch boyfriend. I'm sure I heard my mother's jaw hit the floor, even on the phone thousands of miles away in America.'

Michelle and Erik set about planning her swimming career and his athletics career from their new base. Home in Ireland was a rented house in Celbridge, Co. Kildare, beside their good friend Terry McHugh, the Irish javelin champion and dual Olympian, one of the few Irishmen to represent his country in the summer and winter games thanks to his membership of an historic bobsleigh team.

Terry had met Erik in Seoul and again in Barcelona. He introduced the pair to the joys of the Kildare town a few miles away from Michelle's parents in Rathcoole. Knowing Terry also meant that Erik had a training partner and a friend in a country that knew nothing of his fame or his sporting prowess back in his native Holland.

Erik liked the anonymity when he came to live in Ireland. In Holland, he was a star; in Ireland he was the Dutch boyfriend of the swimmer in the house across the road. Erik liked that. He liked the people. He liked the country.

However, one thing Erik didn't like was the attention his imported sports car drew to their house in commuter-land. Six times joy-riders tried to steal it from outside the house. Eventually, Erik decided enough was enough. He cut down all the trees beside the house, without the landlord's permission. He spread gravel over the back garden. He cleared a space big enough to drive the car around the back of their rented house and away from the prying eyes of those kids on the look-out for a quick thrill behind the wheel of a Dutchman's speed machine. That worked well . . . until the morning Michelle and Erik left at 5 a.m. for her training session in the King's Hospital and the car got stuck in the gravel. The more Erik revved the engine, the more the back wheels became bogged down. They tried everything: they threw towels down, they spun the wheels, but all to no avail.

'The neighbours already thought we were a fairly weird couple because we'd go out training when they were coming in and we'd be coming in when they'd be going out to work,' says Michelle. 'I'm sure that morning just convinced them that the swimmer and her boyfriend were off the wall.'

Michelle and Erik were to leave Ireland in March 1994, the apparent lack of support for her swimming from her national federation and the King's Hospital club forcing them into a move to his native Holland as the next chapter outlines. The move did not put their relationship under pressure. By that stage, they were happily engaged; and in June of this year, they were married in Erik's native village.

Erik takes up the story: 'We got married just a few weeks before the Olympics, at the beginning of June. It felt right to do it then, so we did. We were going to wait until after the Olympics, then we decided to go for it in June. It was a good excuse for us because neither of us wanted a big party. We were going to leave it until after the Olympics but it was a good job we didn't! We were in training for Atlanta and couldn't afford the time to prepare for a wedding, so it was very small and what we both wanted. It was a civil ceremony with both our families present, everything we wanted.'

'We had a great day; and, yes, I did train before and after the wedding,' adds Michelle.

'We got up at 5 a.m. and trained until 8 a.m.,' recalls Erik. 'Then we had breakfast, got changed, went to the registry office and got married – as simple as that. Afterwards we went to my parents' garden and had lunch with them and Michelle's folks. Our honeymoon was in Holland, at the training camp in Florida, and in Atlanta!'

'It was a beautiful day,' adds Michelle, 'it was about 26 degrees and Erik's parents have a beautiful garden. His mother and aunt had prepared a lovely spread. I went to Erik's old bedroom for a sleep in the afternoon, then we went back to the pool and trained from about 6.30 p.m. to 8 p.m. and came back home. It was very relaxing to actually swim on my wedding day. I had been running around all morning so it was nice to have a swim for an hour and a half.'

Erik jokes: 'You were a bit off balance though, you had a ring on one finger!'

That ring of gold received some company in America. But not in the pool itself.

'I do wear my wedding ring all the time but I didn't wear it in the races at the Olympics. Erik wore it around his neck with his accreditation for safe-keeping. At least he didn't lose this ring, but he did manage to lose my engagement ring in Rome, at the World Championships in 1994.'

Erik describes what happened: 'I had these shorts on with a piece of string attached and the key of the hotel room and Michelle's ring on it. So when I went back to the hotel, I opened the string, got the key and went into our room. We only missed it when Michelle asked for the ring. It must have dropped in the hall and the cleaners or someone passing by got it. No, she didn't kill me, but she must have thought about it.'

Michelle de Bruin, as she calls herself these days, and her husband are now inseparable. They have a 24-hour-a-day relationship, a bond that can never be broken.

'How would I describe our relationship? Sure, we fight just like every other couple; but we are close, very close,' says Michelle. Erik agrees. 'We are 24 hours together. If she forgets things, I get a bit annoyed about it, although I do not fight about it.'

'I am an expert at forgetting things,' agrees Michelle and Erik adds, 'You always have to tell her to remember things two or three times.'

And what of the next generation of de Bruins?

'We haven't really thought about children yet – maybe when Michelle is finished swimming. We're agreed that we don't want a big family though; we agreed that one would be enough,' says Erik.

'I'd love one baby and I wouldn't have any problem if the child wanted to be a swimmer. Let him or her go ahead and do whatever he or she wants. In the same way the child can be a footballer, a hurler, tennis player . . . or even a reporter,' laughs Michelle. 'And no, I wouldn't have the baby under water!'

CHAPTER SEVEN

Holland

For 15 months, Michelle Smith and Erik de Bruin lived happily in the County Kildare town of Celbridge, their personal lives as happy as happy could be. Like any young couple in love, their life was idyllic. Professionally, though, all was not well within Irish swimming. The national coach, George Gibney, had fled the country in shame after allegations had been printed in the national media that he had sexually interfered with young swimmers in his charge. Michelle Smith, one of his Olympic protégés, knew nothing of the incidents. She hadn't even heard whispers in the changing-room when the scandal, which had been mainly brought to light by her former Irish team-mate Gary O'Toole, broke.

Michelle says, 'Like the rest of the country, I was deeply shocked. I had no idea that this had allegedly gone on. I had had no personal experience of any such incidents. My sympathy was only with the children concerned and with their families. To abuse trust in a situation like that was unforgivable. And it had far-reaching consequences for swimming. Coaches at international level are now very shy about speaking to young swimmers on a one-to-one basis away from the pools because of what had happened. That is one sad by-product of that scandal. Like everyone involved in swimming, I can have nothing but sympathy for the victims, and nothing but scorn for the perpetrator.'

Life was also troubled for Michelle Smith at the King's Hospital club, a club later to be rocked by its own series of allegations against a top coach, who is now in exile. Her dilemma was purely a training one. She wanted to do her own thing, to devise her own schedule under the watchful eye of her new coach and fiancé. A year earlier, when Erik had moved to Ireland, they had decided that the time was right to put all their eggs into the one basket. He had seen the makings of a champion in his fiancée; she had recognised in him the coach who was going to turn her into a champion.

After a bout of glandular fever had ruined the competitive season in 1993, they formulated their plans for 1994, the World Championships year. They drew up schedules designed to make Michelle Smith a contender in Rome that autumn. Irish swimming did not agree. The IASA wanted Michelle Smith to swim within their confines as part of a national squad adhering to the training schedules of a national coach. The King's Hospital club wanted her to swim their way, in their group, compromising only to the extent that she could do half a programme with Erik and half a programme with her club. Neither body endeared itself to Michelle Smith and Erik de Bruin. So in March of 1994, they left Ireland for the more welcoming shores of Holland, a land that offered the facilities and the freedom to do it their way.

Michelle says quite clearly: 'In early 1994 we were into the World Championships season and I needed access to a 50-metre pool. I also felt a need for independence. Because of the problems at the King's Hospital, I just felt that I wasn't getting enough co-operation from my own club. I wanted to do my own training schedules under Erik's instructions; they wanted me to be part of a group working with Erik and the club coach. That was never going to work.

'In March that year, Erik got the offer of a house to rent near his parents in Hardinxveld, a village of 15,000 people 20 kilometres outside Rotterdam. His dad wasn't well at the time and he wanted to be close to home. It also made absolute sense in terms of the facilities that were going to be available to me to train as a serious swimmer. There was a 50-metre pool 12 minutes away which I joined and there were four or five 25-metre pools within striking distance to ensure that I could have access to all the pool time I needed. The move made sense from every point of view.

'Looking back at it now, it wasn't a hard decision to leave Ireland. At a certain point, we just had to accept that if I was to have a realistic chance at major international events, I couldn't possibly stay in Ireland until a week or so before the games and then expect to do well. It was an easy move to make. Erik had adapted well to Ireland;

he loved the country and the people, but we both knew that his country would offer me a better opportunity to train to the level I wanted to reach. There was no slight on Ireland; it was merely a fact of life.

'There were tough times after the big move, times when it was difficult to adapt. I had undertaken a linguaphone course before I went out, but it was still mind-boggling trying to come to terms with the language barrier. I had learned how to say "please" and "thank you" and "where can I get the number 61 bus?", but all of a sudden I was watching the news and it was all gobbledygook to me. They spoke so fast. It took me about six months before I was able to understand what people were saying.

'There was a big culture difference to get accustomed to as well. Dutch people are mostly very nice people but not as open or as friendly as the Irish. The Dutch are a little more reserved towards people they don't know. And anyway we were still the swimming weirdos next door. We still had little to do with the neighbours or the community as we lived our lives separately and differently. We were up at 5 a.m. to train. When people were going to work we were going back to bed; going out again in the afternoon for more training, then back late in the evenings for dinner and bed. No matter where we had lived we would still have been labelled the weirdos next door.

'However, we still took our ritual Sunday off, breaking that habit only if I needed to catch up on some work in the gym. And quite often on Sundays we would relax at Erik's parents' house, enjoying their hospitality and their garden. That was the only variance from a life dedicated to swimming and training.'

People who know Michelle Smith say that the biggest difference since the move to Holland is in her training. She now trains like no other swimmer, with methods that many will seek to emulate in the light of her Atlanta success. And all this is thanks to one man, one Dutch athlete.

On the first day that Erik de Bruin watched Michelle Smith train at the King's Hospital club in Dublin, he was shocked. Here was a man from the discipline of throwing, used to the rigours of full-time athletics training, watching his fiancée training to become an Olympic contender by swimming up and down the pool in Palmerstown. He watched her going up and down for length after length and he wondered why. Why did they spend their two-hour sessions going through the same pattern of lengths? Why did they not work in the gymnasium on shoulder muscles, stamina, weights and bodybuilding? Why did the coach start the sprint work *after* a couple of hours of going up and down in the same ritual. It didn't make sense.

Just as Michelle Smith had questioned the American coach, Phill Hansell, at Houston University, so Erik questioned her training methods. Something had to change. In March 1994, after Erik de Bruin had moved home to Holland with his fiancée, the real training began. Away from the confines and conflicts of the King's Hospital, Michelle and Erik could make their own plans for her swimming career. Within minutes of their home were training facilities better than anything close at hand back in Dublin. The managers of 25-metre and 50-metre pools only too willing to allow coach and swimmer to undertake whatever programme they wanted on their own. Thus, instead of being one of 25 swimmers working to one coach's programme, Michelle Smith worked to the programme of just one coach – Erik.

Together they planned her routine and her regime. They worked on away from the traditional values of swim coaching. Erik sat down with swim coaches in Holland. He picked their brains. Erik also studied his own sport. He examined where track and field could merge their ideas with the sport of swimming; where Michelle Smith could learn from the ways he had grown accustomed to on his climb up the world ratings. Diet, fitness and regime were earmarked as the key areas for improvement. Michelle's fondness for eating between meals, for snacking, for chocolate, were all quenched.

Erik says, 'I wanted to marry the best of both worlds, the best aspects of swimming and the best aspects of athletics. I knew that there would be a happy medium that could work to Michelle's benefit, that could bring out the potential that was obviously there. For ten years she had trained to false rules and false ways. She needed to change her approach, to change her training, to change her ways. Only then could she swim to her potential. That's what we set about doing.

'Many in the sport will view it as being different, as being radical. But we were true only to our ideals and our dreams. We believe a coach should coach a swimmer in such a way that it comes out of the swimmer himself or herself. The coach should encourage that. So I knew I had to make sure that Michelle did things because she wanted to – that she didn't want to eat biscuits instead of locking them away so that she couldn't.'

Michelle agrees: 'It was about the discipline of the body and the mind. Erik would explain to me why I shouldn't eat certain types of foods; he would explain what foods were better to eat in different combinations. Once I understood the reasoning, I did it myself, I disciplined myself so that it was never a case of waiting until Erik went out and then stuffing myself with five bars of chocolate. To do that would have been to fool myself, nothing else. Instead I learned a lot more about the foods I should eat and the right combinations to assist my training programme.'

Erik also said, 'The key element was her attitude, her desire and her will to win. I was emphasising that a lot more than ever before after we had moved to Holland. When other swimmers from Ireland go to international events they are often in awe of other competitors, even to the extent where some of them ask for autographs at the major championships. If you have that kind of attitude you will never be the winner yourself.'

Immediately after their arrival in Holland, they set about transforming the training programme they both believed had held Michelle Smith back. She was introduced to the local swimming club, Nautilus, the local gym, and the local pool. She was introduced to new ways – individual ways.

Michelle says, 'Even though I was part of a club I was still very much on my own because Erik co-ordinated my training. We trained with the club but I worked entirely under Erik's supervision and programme, in a lane of my own. He was with me at every training session; our only contact with the Nautilus club, aside from training alongside them under Erik's programme, was when I swam with them in leagues and championships. We were very much independent – and very different from tradition.'

Erik explains, 'A coach has to make sure that you do not go up and down, up and down doing lengths all the time. That is not training. The responsibility is on the coach to vary the training. If you have a swimmer doing lengths for five hours he or she will not concentrate. His or her mind will wander to the last meal he or she ate or to his or her last night out. Variety has got to be the spice of life.

'Long training sessions have to be attractive and interesting. That's why our programme is always conducted over ten-day bursts. After that you cannot command concentration from the swimmer. You do short, sharp bursts, and then return to regular training before stepping it up again.'

Michelle concurs: 'That way you are always thinking about something: sometimes focusing more on your technique or your speed; sometimes concentrating on holding certain times. It makes all the difference with Erik at the pool. Instead of having a coach who is trying to look after a group of swimmers, he is looking after me and me alone. He will stand by the pool and tell me my times, tell me what is right and what is wrong. I have instant feedback about my training all the time.'

'Yes,' said Erik. 'It helped Michelle in Atlanta because she had the feeling about how fast she was swimming from our hours in the training pool together. She could judge for herself when she was fast and when she was slow from the time we had spent together working in Holland. If you are a part of a group, you are not told your time when you hit the wall on each turn. The coach can't give you that sort of attention.'

Michelle concludes, 'The attention to detail we have is vital. Sometimes in training Erik will tell me that he wants me to do a certain time or that he wants me to bring my pulse rate up to a certain level. So it gets easier and easier for me then to go out and know what that particular time feels like, rather than for me to come in and wait for him to say, "You're ten seconds off". It helps you in your pacing during races because you have been repeating the pattern of swimming 100 metres and knowing that it was 1:04 or 1:14 or 1:24.

'There is a clock on the wall but we don't use it. I wear my own watch with a second hand to take my pulse rate and Erik has a stopwatch to take all the times. When I come in, I take my pulse rate straightaway and he will record the time; so for every session that we do and for every part of the session, we have times and pulse rates and so much more data than a coach would normally record for his swimmer. When we were training for Atlanta, for example, we knew that I was going to have to be faster than I was before the European Championships last year. We could look back at my training before the European Championships and say well, at this stage two months before the Championships, I was swimming this time for this set with this pulse rate; and then I just had to make sure I was doing better prior to Atlanta.'

Michelle Smith has devoted the last four years of her life to swimming, to the Olympic dream. However, she does have a life outside the pool. 'I like music and reading. I listen to pretty much anything, but I particularly like Mary Black. I'm not really into the house music that's around at the moment. Sometimes in competition I use music as a means of relaxation or to psyche myself up.

'For different events you have to be in different states of mind. For longer events you have to be calm and concentrated and focused on what you want to do in your race and your tactics for swimming the race. In a sprint event, you have to be hyped up and ready to explode off the blocks. It's handy then to use music in that way, to put your headphones on and to have something that is going to blast the ears off you. I had Tina Turner in 1994 for that, something that is very much upbeat. The relaxation tapes would be stuff like Mary Black or Clannad, although I didn't listen to that much in Atlanta.

'I like the cinema as well. Both of us like to go out and have a nice meal and a glass of wine. Neither of us really takes a drink, but we do enjoy a glass of wine when we are not training, at the end of the season. After every six weeks of hard training, we always have a scheduled week's break when we let our hair down a bit.'

That ability to relax has been important for Michelle Smith. Just as Erik de Bruin has altered her diet and training schedule, so he has also altered her rest and relaxation patterns. Michelle says, 'Rest is almost as important as training. I have my rest periods during the day when I am in full-time training and they are vital. But then so is the ability to know when it is time to switch off for a while.

'Erik will know when I have had a really hard week. We did a lot more training this year than in previous years. Sometimes, this year, I went up to 100 kilometres a week in the pool, which takes at least 640 lengths and six hours of swimming every day. After that you just have to let go and relax, and to have something to get away from because you are as tired mentally as you are physically. It tells.

'I do not get moody in the mornings, but I can on occasions be really tired. When you are tired you are not very upbeat or full of energy. That's when I tend to go into myself. The schedule is very tough.

That dedication to duty has served Michelle Smith well these past three years. So has the move to Holland even though she once refused the offer to swim for her husband's country. The Dutch, like the Irish, are proud of their champion.

CHAPTER EIGHT

Rome

It was 1994, the World Cup year. For Jack Charlton and the Irish soccer team in New Jersey and Orlando, it was to be victory against Italy, defeat against Mexico, and a draw with Norway to secure second-phase qualification. Defeat against the Dutch in Orlando: Michelle Smith didn't know which way to look in Hardinxveld. She was a stranger in a strange land that June as Denis Bergkamp and Marc Overmars put paid to Irish ambition.

For Michelle, it was her own 'World Cup' year too – the 'World Cup' championships in swimming: Rome in September. It was to be *arrividerci* anonymity; hello stardom; hello success. That, at least, was the plan as Michelle Smith and her Dutch fiancé set up home in the Netherlands. After all, her short-course season had been successful in the early part of the year when she had won races in the World Championship Cup Grand Prix series both in Paris and Sheffield.

But something was wrong though. Something didn't quite make sense. There was something strange about the lethargy that followed Michelle Smith out of the training pool; there was something curious about her listlessness. All was not well with Michelle when she moved to Holland in the spring of 1994 and she knew it.

Then disaster struck. In April, shortly after the move to Erik's native village, Michelle became ill again, less than a year after glandular fever had ruined her 1993 season. She was lifeless; she was spent. Her resting pulse rate was going up too high after her regular training sessions. A series of tests failed to provide the answers, the Dutch doctors merely ascertaining that there was a virus active in her immune system. For most people, that would have necessitated a complete rest, a break from the stress and strain of everyday life. For Michelle Smith, it spelt only bad news, just four months before the World Championships in Rome.

Michelle shuddered. 'It was the worst thing that could have happened to me. Everything that season had been geared to make a breakthrough at the World Championships. I had wintered well, coming back into active competition with some good World Cup Championship times, particularly in France and England. I was already making plans for the summer, and intending to do altitude training with Erik in Font Romeu in the south of France instead of going to Arizona with the rest of the Irish team, as the IASA had suggested. My Dutch club colleague, Inge de Bruijn, the European bronze medallist for the 100-metre butterfly, had been to Font Romeu and had recommended it for long-course training in the build-up to the World Championships. But I never got near the south of France. Instead I ended up going no further than the nearest pool in Holland. The virus refused to go away until just eight weeks before the World Championships. I had had no energy, no recovery levels, no vitality for three months. It was so frustrating. Even while the virus was active, I had tried to stay in some sort of shape with work-outs in both the pool and the gym, but still I was drifting around in a constant state of exhaustion.'

Eight weeks before the September finals in Rome, Michelle Smith began to feel better. Her pulse rate was down; her energy levels were up. After a lot of talking, Michelle and Erik decided to push the training routine for six weeks, before taking a decision on her fitness and entry for the 200-metre and 400-metre individual medleys and the 100-metre and 200-metre butterfly. Two weeks before the World Championships Michelle Smith and Erik decided to go ahead with her entry for Rome.

As it happened, the IASA had copied a trend set by the Spanish Federation at the Barcelona Olympics when they entered swimmers with times far greater than anything they had achieved. Thus Michelle Smith had been entered for the 400-metre individual medley with a time of 4:44, more than 12 seconds better than her best long-course time set at the World Championships in Perth in 1991.

In Rome, Michelle swam on the first day of competition for the heats of the 400-metre individual medley. Despite the after-effects of her illness, Michelle swam the race of her life, coming in third in the heat in a time of 4:50.32, and smashing her long-course Irish record of three years' standing. Her heat was won by one Alison Wagner of America, with J. Malar of Canada second. Remember the name, 'Wagner'.

Michelle's heroics on that opening day were not enough to gain her a place in the 400-metre individual medley final. Instead she finished ninth fastest and had to be content with a place in the 'B' final.

She ruled the roost in that 'B' final, dismissing the threat of New Zealand's Anne Wilson and Japan's Mitomi Maemara in the second leg of the backstroke to win in a time of 4:47.89, trimming a total of nine seconds off her Irish record between heat and final in the course of her day's work.

Wagner was to win silver in the 'A' final, having been beaten by the Chinese girl, Dai Guohong, with a fellow American, Kristine Quance, third. Their paths were to cross again two years later. For now though, Michelle, Erik and her parents who were present at the poolside, could rejoice in the 'B' final victory that meant so much for a swimmer clearly off top form.

Michelle says: 'Winning that "B" final was a breakthrough for me. I had been bitterly disappointed to miss out on the "A" final by such a narrow margin in the heats. To win the "B" final and earn a ninth spot in the world rankings made up for it.'

She made the 'B' final for the 100-metre butterfly and 200-metre individual medley but opted out of both to reserve her energy for the 200-metre butterfly. She wanted to make an 'A' final to finish in the top eight in the world. Split times in the 100-metre butterfly and the 200-metre individual medley also yielded new Irish records for the Dublin girl. In the 100-metre butterfly, Michelle finished 16th fastest in the heats, and withdrew from the 'B' final to save her energy for the 200-metre butterfly. It was to be a wise choice.

Michelle Smith reserved the best till last. She made history on the final day of the World Championships, the first Irish swimmer to reach a World Championships final. In the process, she finished fifth in the final of the 200-metre butterfly, smashing Marion Madine's Irish record in both the heats and the finals. Her qualification for the final alone ranked as an amazing achievement, likened by one Irish official in Rome to Christy O'Connor Junior playing on a pitch and putt course in Ireland and then winning the US Open on a championship golf course, his analogy for the lack of a 50-metre facility in Ireland.

In the heat, Michelle smashed the Irish record as she recorded the fourth fastest time of the day. In the final itself she had to be content with fifth spot in a race dominated, as the championships had been all week, by the Chinese. Their swimmers, Liu Limin and Qu Yun, came in one and two, with Australia's Susan O'Neill third, and Denmark's Mette Jacobsen fourth. No one, though, could take from the achievement of Michelle Smith, Ireland's first world championship race finalist. By the end of that week in Rome, Michelle had broken eight Irish records and rewritten the history books when she qualified for the final in a new Irish record time of 2:13.22, before breaking it again with a time of 2:12.79 for her fifth spot in that final.

Michelle concludes: 'It was a great World Championships. If I had avoided the illness beforehand, who knows what might have happened. What was important for me, though, was the fact that I had turned the corner in terms of my achievements. I had taken the benefits of my new training programme and put them to work in the pool. Fifth in the 200-metre butterfly was my best result to date. I also won the "B" final in the 400-metre individual medley and just missed out on the "A" final at a time when I didn't really have any endurance training behind me.

'The butterfly was the real bonus. My stroke had been getting better for me in training so I decided to enter the race without expecting to make the final. I qualified fourth fastest going into the final and ended up coming fifth, just three one-hundredths of a second behind the girl who was fourth. It was the beginning of the upturn in my fortunes as far as I am concerned.'

In the course of 1994, Michelle Smith's name appeared 26 times for Irish records set in the 200-metre and 400-metre individual medley; the 200-metre backstroke; the 50-metre, 100-metre and 200-metre butterfly; and, for the first time, in the 50-metre, 800-metre and 1,500-metre freestyle events. She was ranked fifth in the world over the 400-metre individual medley short course and ninth in the world over the long course after the World Championships, where she also finished fifth in the 200-metre butterfly ratings. And she was rated 12th in the world in both the 100-metre butterfly and the 200-metre individual medley.

It had been a good year for Michelle Smith, illness or no illness. She had found a base for her training in Holland, she had developed a system with Erik to match her determination. It was looking good as they looked to the future: Vienna for the 1995 European Championships and Atlanta for the 1996 Olympic games.

Michelle agrees: 'Even with my illness it has to go down as a good year, as a year of improvement. I noticed the physical change in my form in January and February when I went to the World Cup Championships meetings in Paris and Sheffield. My form had risen appreciably in the short course earlier in the year and I was beginning to rise in the world rankings. It had been hard work, but it was paying off. I came out of the World Championships in 1994 knowing that my swimming had considerably improved.

'I suppose it was at that stage that I started looking towards Atlanta, but I was more focused on the short term and my prospects for the European Championships. Erik never made any promises. He said we would just work at the programme and see how things unfolded. He is not the sort of coach to promise world titles or gold medals simply for sticking to a programme.'

Erik says: 'No, I would never make promises. I think it is very dangerous, especially with children aged 13 or 14, to make such promises to them. What happens if the child doesn't make it? You always have to be very careful as a coach when making promises.'

Michelle continued: 'After the World Championships there was only one European, Mette Jacobsen from Denmark, who was ahead of me in the 200-metre butterfly. She beat me by three one-hundredths of a second and I never heard the end of that for an entire year from Erik! But that was good as well for me because it gave me that extra little bit of encouragement – the margin of difference she had beaten me by was so small! I didn't want to be beaten again!'

Erik picked up the story. 'We then began to develop the training methods, to look at other ways in which we could adopt athletics coaching for swimming. With the gap so narrow between Michelle and the best girl in Europe, there was now real hope that she could go to Vienna the following year and win a medal. It was important to start again after Rome; to reassess the programme and draw up a two-year plan to take Michelle all the way to the Olympic finals. We knew what had to be done now. And we knew how we wanted to do it.

'I felt that there were a lot of ways that weights in particular could help Michelle. After Rome, I really went to work on that. A friend of mine has a velocity meter that helps in the pool work-outs in the pool, and we also acquired a bio robot, which is a computer that measures the speed at which you move the bar in your weight-training in the gym. When you move weights, it's important not just how heavy the weights are but also the speed at which you are moving them. That counts too: if you have 30 kilogrammes which you move really fast, the weight "becomes" more than 30 kilogrammes. If you look at the way you are swimming and how quickly your muscles are contracting, then you should look to a similar weight programme and assimilate that. However, you cannot measure it just by looking; you need to use a computer which can tell you either to slow down or pick up in case you are going too quickly or slowly. It also makes sure you train a lot more efficiently.'

Michelle added: 'We can also do underwater stroke analysis with the velocity meter. A video camera analyses my angles and speeds through the computer, then it compares it with those of other swimmers.'

All that was to work in Michelle Smith's favour. 1994 had counted as a good year, but there were better to come. Unfortunately, money was still a thorny subject. When Michelle Smith returned home for a brief visit after her conquests in Rome, she told the Irish media of her urgent need for financial support from any quarter. Government funding for Michelle, via the Olympic Council and Cospoir, had increased to £7,000. The Chinese, in stark comparison, had invested a cool million in the swimmers who had reaped a gold medal harvest at the Rome games.

Michelle remembers: 'After Rome, I was still low in the income support bracket, with somewhere between £3,000 and £7,000 coming from the Cospoir grant fund and the OCI, at a time when we were paying £20 an hour in Holland just for pool rental. We needed assistance from some quarter.'

That assistance was to be found just around the corner as Michelle Smith carried the form of 1994 into the new season. She was about to make her pitch for status as a suitable recipient for one of the Olympic Council's élite sports persons grants worth between £15,000 and £20,000 a year. Also, a sponsor was about to enter the fray.

CHAPTER NINE

Vienna

Rome was a distant memory at the start of the 1995 season. Michelle Smith and Erik de Bruin had settled into a routine at their Dutch home. Together they worked on the masterplan that was destined to strike a rich vein of form in the Georgian waters 18 months later. Together they worked on a training schedule to maximise her potential at the European Championships in Vienna that August. Together they worked on a schedule to ensure that the heartache of Barcelona and Rome was never again to be repeated.

The year commenced with an assault on the World Cup programme that began with a January trip to Hong Kong. The World Cup was one of the bones of contention between Michelle and the Irish swimming association, the IASA. They contended that she was only entitled to participate in their funding programme if she participated in their plan for the national squad for the year under the auspices of the national director of swimming, David McCullough, at a time when the post of national coach was still vacant. He tried to accommodate them but he too was answerable to the IASA and the World Cup was not a part of the IASA programme for 1995.

Michelle and Erik eventually agreed to disagree with the IASA. She had to compete in the World Cup as far as they were concerned. The sport's governing body in Ireland didn't agree and refused to send her to Hong Kong at their expense. Michelle went anyway, without her coach. Finances were so tight in the de Bruin household that she went to the Far East on her own. Her only companion at the poolside was the Filipino swimmer Christina Bautista, a classmate from their university days together in Houston.

Without Erik in Hong Kong, Michelle was a lost soul out of the pool. In it, she missed his instructive gaze from the poolside, but not his influence. The hours of training began to pay off. She knew the way to win the 200-metre butterfly in the World Cup. She knew the way Erik wanted her to perform in the welcoming waters of Hong Kong. And she did exactly as she was told. The doubts of Rome and Barcelona were extinguished as Michelle Smith swept to victory in the 200-metre and 100-metre butterfly in Hong Kong, a prelude to her overall victory at those distances in that year's World Cup.

Ireland, a land that had greeted her performances in Seoul, Barcelona and Rome with little more than respectful disregard, sat up and took notice. Her father, Brian, was asked onto the Gay Byrne radio show and told the nation how he caught up on lost sleep in the back of his van outside the King's Hospital pool as a young Michelle trained for the stardom to come. He spoke too of her circumstances as a full-time athlete, without full-time support, in faraway Holland. He revealed how her chance meeting with Erik de Bruin at the tail-end of the Barcelona Olympics had changed not just her life but her swimming. And he told the nation how Michelle had to pay her own way to the World Cup meet in Hong Kong because Irish swimming did not see it as a meritable part of her build-up to the world short-course season and then the European Championships.

Brian Smith touched hearts when he told how Michelle had travelled halfway across the world without her coach, her fiancé and her confidant because of her lack of finance. And for one man, listening in corporate Dublin, it was the catalyst to a relationship that has been nothing short of wonderful for both swimmer and sponsor. Geoff Carr, managing director of the giant TNT Express Worldwide operation at Dublin Airport, was left with a sense of disbelief as he heard Brian Smith tell of his daughter's plight on the national airwaves after her Hong Kong exploits. He decided to do something about it. He made contact with the Smith camp and one of the most successful athlete–sponsor relationships in the history of Irish sport was underway.

Michelle takes up the story: 'Geoff and TNT came on board in January 1995, just after I had won the first competition for the World Cup short-course season out in Hong Kong, as I was preparing for the start of the European leg of the competition closer to home. He had heard my father explain on the radio how I had to go out to the

Far East on my own as we could not afford the considerable cost for both of us to go. In normal circumstances, the swimmers' Federation pays for their teams to go out, but I had to fund myself. I had requested funding from the IASA for Hong Kong and had been refused. They had had their own programme for that year. Hong Kong was not a part of their programme; so, because I wanted to do something else, I had to fund it from my own resources. I tried to explain to them that I was going out there because I felt comfortable about my prospects. They didn't listen.'

'The Federation just didn't take her seriously when we made the approach for funding for Hong Kong,' adds Erik. 'They just did not think she could win it.'

Michelle continues: 'The outlay for my ticket was worth it. I won the butterfly category which is a combination of the 100 metres and 200 metres. I picked up the maximum 20 points available in the World Cup rankings for the butterfly event in Hong Kong and that left me in a very advantageous position going into the European legs. Some swimmers opted to compete only in the three European legs which gave me a big head start in the race for the World Cup title.'

Victory was lonely though. Without Erik as her coach for the first time in a competitive environment, Michelle had to draw deep on her own resolve and ambition. They were never to be parted at the pool again.

'It was tough without Erik, even for that short length of time. We had come to rely on each other and now we were apart. The only person I had there for me was my best friend at college, Christina from the Philippines, who was working in Hong Kong at the time. She was my surrogate coach; she came along to the competition with me and did the sort of routine things that Erik looked after, like taking my splits. It was good just to have a friend there, someone to talk to, someone to bounce off, someone to go to dinner with.'

Erik agrees: 'It was tough for Michelle out there and for me back home in Holland; but like everything else in life, there was a positive side to it. A coach should ensure that the swimmer can cope on his or her own. You do not want to create somebody who is dependent on you all the time. The swimmer or the athlete must be able to cope without the coach. That is almost as important as coaching and being there with your athlete.'

In the modern world of sport, the sponsor is oft times as valuable as the coach. Michelle Smith went to Hong Kong without a coach or a sponsor. She came back with new recognition, a proud coach waiting at Amsterdam Airport, and a sponsor waiting in Dublin in the guise of an Englishman who once played soccer eight times for his native Sunderland.

'Geoff heard my dad on radio saying that I hadn't got a sponsor and explaining that I really needed one in preparation for the Europeans,' explains Michelle. 'He immediately made contact with my dad and said that he could not believe that I had to pay my own fare out to Hong Kong. He has been really good to me ever since. Within a fortnight of my return from that World Cup meeting, I had met Geoff, together with my agent at the time, and a deal was done.

'On the day we announced the deal in Dublin, he just said to me that I was under no pressure to produce results, only to do my best. Geoff wasn't to know then that I would go on and win medals in Vienna or Atlanta; yet he was prepared to put his company's money into my future there and then. That is something that I will always cherish. His company was there for me when very few people wanted to know.

'TNT and I have had a policy from the start that we will not discuss the money that TNT has invested, but I can say without fear of contradiction that Geoff and his company have been more than good to me. The sponsorship gave us more security in our preparations for the European Championships. At that stage I was still awaiting classification as one of the Olympic élite athletes under the Olympic Council of Ireland grants scheme. TNT were there when we needed someone.'

That security served Michelle Smith well in the weeks and months leading up to the European Championships in Vienna. As her momentum was maintained under the watchful eye of Erik de Bruin, so her times improved. She completed the World Cup series with outright victory by accumulating sufficient points in the butterfly, which resulted in a world short-course ranking in May 1995 of number one for the 200-metre butterfly, number six for the 100-metre butterfly, and number seven for the 200-metre individual medley. She also continued her assault on the record books with 19 Irish records for the season, including new records in the 100-metre and 200-metre freestyle as her technique and style continued to reap the benefits of her new training regime and her lifestyle in Holland.

All she did was carefully geared towards the European Championships in Vienna and one more chance to finally show the world that Michelle Smith of Ireland was a force to be reckoned with on the biggest stages of them all. In June of 1995, she swam the Dutch national championships, risking the ire of the officials in the process as she swam a time for the 400-metre individual medley that was only five seconds outside her then personal best. Unfortunately she also swam the individual medley in the 400-metre freestyle final at the national championships. The Dutch were not amused but Michelle and Erik ignored the controversy, happy in the knowledge that their plan was bang on course for Vienna.

Michelle explains: 'Before the European Championships I wanted to swim the Dutch nationals, but I didn't want my times going into the world rankings before Vienna; I wanted to keep my times a surprise for the competition. So I entered for the 400-metre freestyle and I swam the 400-metre medley. They got a bit peeved off with that. Instead of swimming the 400-metre freestyle I swam the 100-metre butterfly, the 100-metre backstroke, the 100-metre breaststroke, 100-metre freestyle. One or two coaches got annoyed about it and said I was being unsportsman-like. They gave out to Erik but I suspect there was a little bit of jealousy there.'

By the time Michelle Smith set off for the European Championships she was ready to take on the best Europe could offer – and win. First on her Vienna programme was the 400-metre individual medley. Michelle Smith was ranked number two on the start list thanks to a personal best set in the B-final at the World Championships in Rome a year earlier. Ominously, at number one in the rankings, was the the great Hungarian Krizstina Egerszeggi, unbeaten in the event throughout her career, an Olympic champion at 13 and the most feared swimmer over the distance in the world. When Egerszeggi entered the 400-metre individual medley she did so because she knew she was going to win. She did not enter races she was worried about.

The heats went well for the Rathcoole girl. She knocked four seconds off her personal best, easing down in the final 100 metres as she qualified fastest for the final. Egerszeggi looked less comfortable on her way to that final, the European champion's form a cause for concern in her camp.

Michelle Smith, as ever, led from the front in the final, before a capacity crowd at the Ernshappel Stadium. She took off like a rocket, leading after a very fast first 100 metres butterfly in 62.42 seconds. Egerszeggi , though, was just seven-hundredths of a second behind Smith and going into her favourite backstroke leg. By the halfway mark, she had built up an impregnable five-second lead. Michelle Smith's butterfly had not been strong enough to guarantee the gold medal but she had made a great attempt for it. By the end of the breaststroke, she had the Hungarian's lead down to just three seconds. By the final 100-metre freestyle leg, she was still battling, eventually losing by just two and a half seconds to the three-time Euro champion in a time of 4:42.81, a time that was the second best in the world that year, a time that could have been better.

At the post-race press conference, Egerszeggi paid tribute to Michelle's improvement. 'I was more than aware of Michelle Smith in the race,' proclaimed the Budapest restaurateur. 'I did not know a lot about her but I knew I had to go out hard to stay with her on the butterfly leg. At that point, I realised that I could win. My breaststroke is my weakest leg, so I had to build up a good lead on the backstroke to get away from Smith.'

Michelle Smith said after the race that she was more than happy with the silver medal. With hindsight, she knows now that it could have been closer. She knew then that it would get closer between the pair in the future.

'I knew as I was going into the final that there was nobody in the world near Egerszeggi when it came to the backstroke. I had to be strong in the butterfly because she had studied my heat that morning and knew that the butterfly was my strong point. I thought, going into the final, that I still had a bit to give in the freestyle, but it was the butterfly that was going to make or break me in that first 100 metres. To be fair to her she kept up with me in the butterfly and then she tried to gain as much as she possibly could on the backstroke. I knew she was going to try that, so I was looking around, worrying about how much she was going to gain on me instead of thinking about my own backstroke leg. It was a mistake to think about where Egerszeggi was and not concentrate on my own technique. I ended up swimming a slower backstroke leg – by a second – than I had done in the heat that morning. Nevertheless, that gave me confidence: she had only beaten me by two and a half seconds. I knew I could make ground on Egerszeggi after that race.

And to start the European Championships with a silver after all the disappointments in Barcelona and Rome was not a bad start to the events – not bad at all.'

Irish celebrations afterwards only served to breed confidence that Michelle Smith would follow her silver medal with a gold in the 100-metre butterfly three days later. After all, as the fastest qualifier in a time of 1:00.59, she had already broken the Irish record for 50 metres and 100 metres; and, now, her speed fuelled those flames of ambition. But it was not to be. The final ended in a blanket finish with split seconds separating the first five. Smith was credited with fifth place in a time that was almost a second slower than her heat. Her split time was down on the heat, as Denmark's Mette Jacobsen won her second European Championship gold in a time of 1:00.64.

Michelle recalls the events: 'The 100-metre butterfly was a total disaster; I made the same mistake as I had done in the 400-metre individual medley. I did not escape with a medal this time. I had qualified first for the final with the fastest time of the day, a time that was to prove to be the fastest time in the championships. But all that did was to inspire the wrong ideas. Going into the final, I realised for the first time that I had the chance of winning a gold medal at international level. That unsettled me. I dove into the water and immediately started to look towards the Danish girl, Mette Jacobsen, on my left-hand side. I kept watching to see where she was and forgot about my own race.

'I ended finishing fifth in a race I should have won. It was a painful lesson. My coach told me I was stupid. He was right.'

Erik explains: 'I told Michelle that what she had just learned in that 100-metre butterfly was going to be more important to her than all the medals when she prepared to go to the Olympics in Atlanta. And it was true.'

It was a hard message to accept for the girl from Rathcoole who was riding on the back of the silver medal high she had just experienced three days earlier. But it was a lesson that was going to pay handsome dividends in the future.

'Erik was right. Being placed fifth and losing that medal in the manner in which I lost it was more instrumental to my winning the two European golds after that, and then the medals in Atlanta, than anyone can possibly understand. The lesson was to stand me in good stead for a long time to come.'

It was also to benefit Michelle in the short term. Irish experts on site in Vienna advised Michelle through the media to skip the 200-metre individual medley and concentrate on the 200-metre butterfly, traditionally her strongest event. She thought about it, but she declined their advice. Instead, she listened to her coach who told her to go for it. She did; and she was right.

'The fact that I had the 200-metre individual medley the day after the 100-metre butterfly was a double-edged sword. It was difficult to get back into it after the nature of that loss, but we sat down over a cappuccino that evening and discussed the race from start to finish. Erik told me that I knew what I had done wrong; and he urged me to bounce back from it the next day, and to show that I had learnt the lessons of that defeat when I got back into the water in the 200-metre individual medley. He illustrated the need for concentration with a story about his 1990 European Championship experience – how he hadn't realised how beautiful the stadium in Split had been until he got back to Holland and watched a video of the event with his father. That was how focused he was. He told me I had to be as focused as that in the pool, that nothing around me should interfere with my preparation. We decided to go for it.'

It was the right choice. Inspired by Erik's words of wisdom, she distanced herself from the events of the Friday night when she got back into the pool on Saturday morning for the 200-metre individual medley heats. She qualified as the fastest of the eight, later admitting that had she been the slowest qualifier she would have withdrawn from the final. It was to prove an irrelevant piece of information.

Michelle Smith's hopes in that final were strengthened when a strongly fancied German, Daniella Hunger, the 1988 Olympic champion, and the Russian champion failed to make it. Her biggest threat came from the Belgian, Brigitte Becue, who had already won the 100-metre and 200-metre breaststroke golds in Vienna.

It was a close call between the pair in Ernshappel Stadium. Smith fully utilised her skills on the butterfly and backstroke to give herself a three-second advantage before Becue's trump card, the breaststroke leg. But it was too much for the Belgian to make up. Michelle Smith won the final in an Irish record time of 2:15.27, the second fastest time in the world that year. She also clocked up additional best times on the opening 50-metre butterfly legs in both the heat and the final, two of the eight Irish records she was to smash in Austria.

The wedding of Brian Smith and Patricia Traynor, 4 January 1969.

ABOVE: Michelle at school standing in front of the head teacher (in white polo neck). Michelle is the one with pig tails.

RIGHT: Michelle's first Holy Communion Day 1979. *Left to right:* Paul (cousin), Michelle, Sarah.

The Smith family on Sarah's Communion Day.
Left to right: Michelle, Pat, Sarah, Aisling, Brian.

Michelle in 1985 with a collection of trophies including the Larry Williamson Trophy for 'Top Swimmer at National Championships' and 'Leinster Swimmer of the Year'.

Wedding Day, 11 June 1996. *Above:* Erik and Michelle with brother Brian and *below:* with the Registrar Mrs Bakker.

RIGHT: In the King's Hospital Pool 1985.

At home in Rathcoole: *left to right* Sarah,
Erik, Michelle, Aisling.

Atlanta 1996. *Above:* Michelle in the 400m Individual Medley and *below:* in the 400m Freestyle.

'That Saturday morning,' Michelle recalls, 'I had to get my head together after the disappointment of the previous day and try to swim a good race. In the morning, I swam well; well enough to make the final as the fastest qualifier. I remember now that there were a couple of swimmers who should have done well and didn't. There was a German girl who was European champion, and another, a Russian, who had a very fast time prior to that. They were both knocked out in the heats so I knew then that I had a chance of winning a medal. This time I concentrated in the final on swimming my own race, not bothering with anyone else or thinking of what they were doing. I did not look around at any stage, even though on the last 50 metres freestyle it was tempting to sneak a look. I kept my head down and kept going without knowing my placing until I had touched the wall. Some reporters, I think it was RTE's John Kenny, said to me afterwards that I looked almost surprised when I saw on the scoreboard that I had won. I literally didn't have any idea of where I was. It took a few moments for me to turn around to see on the scoreboard that I was European champion less than 24 hours after I had blown a gold medal. I had been so focused on the race after that disappointment that I didn't even realise I had won it.

'When I saw "number one" against my name, it was a great feeling, a feeling that I will never forget. I was ecstatic, emotional, delirious. I went over to the side of the pool, and Erik was the same – he was crying.

'He had told me before the race to apply tunnel vision, to think only of my own swim. He pointed out that the electronic scoreboard would tell me how good I was. I followed his instructions to the letter. My concentration was so intense that I almost forgot to look up to see my time after touching the finishing pads.

'When I look back on my swimming career, that will rank as the best European medal of them all. Winning the silver in Vienna was special; winning gold in Atlanta was unbelievable. But, as with winning at the Olympics nothing, in terms of the Europeans, will ever compare with winning that first gold medal, that first major championship victory in Vienna. The first gold at the Europeans, as at the Olympics, was the greatest.'

There was more to come. Michelle Smith celebrated her first gold medal with a mineral water and her husband for company. Her family couldn't make it to Austria as Michelle's mother, Pat, was in

Lourdes on a pre-arranged pilgrimage for the first half of the European programme. Her prayers were answered that Saturday, as Michelle's proud parents, Brian and Pat, watched back in the family local, the Poitín Still in Rathcoole, with Aisling and young Brian. Brian senior had a glass of whiskey in his hand and almost dropped it in his excitement. The next day, Sunday, more prayers, more whiskey, more excitement and more gold followed for the Smith family.

The 200-metre butterfly had long been recognised as a Michelle Smith speciality. The pressure had eased on Saturday night when she became the first Irish swimmer to win gold at a major championship. But it did not ease her own expectations. Now, she would set world-record-class pace at all three splits, coming in at 29.44, 1:02.24 and 1:35.91. In the final 50 metres her tired limbs gave way to a world record attempt; they did not give way to the pursuit of gold.

Dublin's pride stormed to victory in 2:11.60 ahead of Denmark's Mette Jacobsen, her 100-metre butterfly conqueror, and her compatriot, Sophia Skou. The highly rated French girl, Cecile Jeanson, was left trailing in Michelle's wake, finishing only fourth.

'Even though I had gold and silver medals behind me I had to put them to the back of my mind for the 200-metre butterfly final on the last day of the competition in Vienna. I had to do the same then as in Atlanta and carry on regardless of what had gone on before. There was added pressure because this was the race which people expected me to do best in, because of the medal results prior to it and because of the fact that I had won the butterfly section of the World Cup series at the beginning of '95. My 200-metre butterfly times had been good, but only Erik and I knew how hard the week's competition had been with three big races back to back on the Friday, Saturday and Sunday.

'Again, the plan was to concentrate on my own race, to ignore Jacobsen who had already won the 100-metre butterfly and 100-metre backstroke that week, and to make sure that I lived up to my standing as the fastest flyer over the first 100 metres. Everything went according to plan up to 150 metres. I had a half second advantage over the two Danes at 50 metres, 1.7 seconds at 100 metres and a full two seconds at 150 metres. Then Jacobsen made her move; and, in the last 50 metres, I just started to die. My stroke started getting very short but I knew I had enough left in me to go on, to dig deep and win. Thankfully I did just that. And, yes, my win did bring on another few tears.

'I don't normally cry after events; I think it is the mixture of excitement and nerves that holds me back. But I cried at the end of both Vienna and Atlanta. It was more a release of all the stress that had been building up than an emotional dam being burst. Those gold medals really meant something.'

Michelle Smith left Vienna with golds in the 200-metre butterfly and the 200-metre individual medley, and a silver in the 400-metre individual medley. She described that first gold medal in the 200-metre individual medley as the best. It was not the last; proving to a cynical world that Michelle Smith did not spring out of nowhere before Atlanta, a fact which she is still keen to point out.

'At the end of the season, my times in the 200-metre individual medley and the 400-metre individual medley in Vienna were both second in the world rankings, so they had been fast races. I have had this gradual improvement throughout the past few years in my performances which is why I was annoyed with the perception at Atlanta where people believed I had come out of nowhere.'

'I can understand people questioning her improvement in the 400-metre freestyle,' adds Erik. 'Last year she did not swim a fast 400-metre freestyle. But in the 400-metre individual medley she did not improve that much on her 1995 time. In the 200-metre individual medley she had improved by 1.3 seconds, which is not a lot when you look at some of the others who had improved by up to five seconds. But the Americans were still playing games there, saying that Michelle had not been in the top 70 last year when she was number two in two events. Either they are very stupid, which I don't think they are, or they had manipulated the plain facts.'

'At that stage in Vienna, there were no accusations,' says Michelle. 'People were just curious about how I had changed and what I was doing in my training. They asked questions about our training routines back in Holland – legitimate questions that received legitimate answers.'

Erik explains: 'We have a strategy that if we are going to a major championship, Michelle doesn't swim fast beforehand. Where is the point in that? There are only medals to be won at the Europeans and the Olympics. Of course, if you look at the Americans, they have to do trials; we don't have to do that. Michelle qualified for the

Olympics a year in advance, and she did the same for the Europeans. The Americans swam faster at the trials than Michelle's winning time in the Olympics. So I would say to the Americans don't point your finger at Michelle, point your finger at yourself and say, "Oh yeah, I swam really badly." If you swam 2:13 at your trials and then 2:17 at the Olympics then I would say that there is definitely something wrong with you.'

CHAPTER TEN

Almost There

Vienna brought out that well-known Irish sporting champion, the back-slapper, followed in hot pursuit by the assistance that had been long overdue as Michelle Smith was finally granted the status of élite athlete by the Olympic Council of Ireland. On her brief visit home after the European Championship gold medal, Michelle Smith was the subject of much gratification from the politicians of Ireland, the same people who had promised so much to so many and delivered so little when it came to real sporting achievement and investment. The funding was a different matter as the public sector finally decided to take a leaf out of Geoff Carr's book at TNT and put some money where all those politicians' mouths were.

According to Michelle, 'In the build-up to the Atlanta games, the Olympic Council of Ireland selected a team of athletes that they felt had a good chance of doing well at the Olympics. I was included in that team for the allocation of one of the grants of between £10,000 and £20,000. It is not enough to get you through the whole year but it does help. I received that for the 1995/96 season, on the back of the successes at Vienna, and it did make a difference.

'As regards the politicians jumping on the bandwagon, that doesn't bother me anymore, although I guess at one stage it did. There was always somebody standing behind you during the glory moments; but I know, and I think the public knows, that all the hard work was put in by Erik and me. I have no problem though with Mary Robinson. She is a woman I admire greatly. It has been nothing short of a pleasure to meet our President. When she welcomed me home at Dublin Airport I was in such a state of elation that I still can't remember what she said to me.'

In the aftermath of the European Championships, recognition came Michelle Smith's way, followed almost immediately by expectation. The talk turned to gold medals in the next stage of competitive swimming, the Olympic stage.

Michelle remembers: 'After a quick visit home to Ireland following Vienna, we returned to Holland and went straight back into training. People were beginning to say that I had a chance of winning a medal in Atlanta, so it was good that I was at home in Holland and removed from that. I knew that once the European Championships was over, the hard work would really only begin. We knew it would not be good enough for me to do the same times in Atlanta as I had done in Vienna; the times would have to be much better. So it was really a tall order for people to say at that point in time that I was guaranteed a gold medal at the Olympics. Luckily I wasn't at home at the time, I wasn't exposed to that sort of pressure.

'Vienna was a sure sign that the changes in my training techniques and Erik's coaching were beginning to have an affect. I knew in Rome that things were getting better; but that meeting had been tainted by my illness that year and glandular fever the year earlier. It was the lack of real training that had curtailed my times in Italy.

'Vienna was a different story. Over the years, I had always been a good distance swimmer but without the speed. All my training, all those hours going up and down in straight lines in the King's Hospital pool had prepared me to stay in the water longer than anyone else. What Erik did was to combine my stamina with speed. That's the biggest difference in my stroke now, as a comparison between my times at the European Championships and the Olympics will verify.

'In America, my 400-metre individual medley came down by three seconds, and my 200-metre individual medley came down by 1.3 seconds; my 200-metre butterfly came down by 1.6 or 1.7 seconds, and the 100-metre butterfly which I did in Vienna was something I just didn't do in Atlanta.'

Michelle and Erik didn't just work on her speed. They also worked on her mind: the power of positive thinking. A positive mental attitude was to be more important in Atlanta than at any other stage of her development as a top-class swimmer. Coach and athlete knew that in the months that followed Vienna as Atlanta beckoned.

As Michelle says, 'The Olympics are about one thing and one thing only – winning medals. Everything else is incidental – absurd almost. At a lot of the other championships, people break world records or they swim very fast times. But in swimming, very often the winning times in the Olympics are not spectacular as it is more about racing to win medals than breaking speed records. I knew I would have to be sharper again in America than I was for the Europeans, but I really didn't care if my time was five seconds faster or slower than in Vienna if I came away with a medal from the Olympics. There are other times when you will go for a record or fast time; but at the major championships it is about winning medals.

'That positive mental attitude was so important for me; it was a point Erik kept driving home. I cannot speak for other sports; but, in swimming, a lot of the time the people who are the favourites going into the games do not win. That happens frequently, as it did in America, because the pressure on them has been too much. They end up performing below the standard they are capable of, which is enough to lose them a medal. That can explain why sometimes people come out of absolutely nowhere and win medals at the Olympics and World Championships.'

Vienna was almost a year before Atlanta. For that interim period, Michelle and Erik worked and trained, nothing more and nothing less. They trained twice a day for six days a week in 25-metre and 50-metre pools in Holland. They allowed themselves a rest on Sundays, often going for a quiet meal with a relaxing glass of wine – always only one glass of wine. They adjourned occasionally to the cinema. And they trained some more.

In the immediate aftermath of Vienna, Michelle did go home occasionally. She worked for Geoff Carr and TNT; she appeared on the *Pat Kenny Show*. She won a Texaco sports star award. And then, at the end of January 1996, she pulled down the shutters and cut out the public insight into her life. Michelle Smith and Erik de Bruin had started the countdown to Atlanta on 1 February. And practically nothing got in their way.

Michelle's last interview was with RTE's Tommy Gorman at her home in Holland. She recalls, 'Tommy is based in Belgium, so he came across the border with a camera crew to do a piece in our own environment as a build-up to Atlanta in Olympic year. As it happened, my parents were over with us at the time and he did a piece on me at a competition and then at home with the two of us. We had our matching Arran jumpers on for the camera! Erik's still laughing about that because I did a job on his jumper in the washing machine afterwards and it ended up a rather small size.'

'So now she has two the same size!' says Erik.

That television appearance and the media coverage that had followed Michelle Smith's Viennese victory served to heighten her public profile in Ireland, but to no great extent. As she says, 'When we came home from Vienna, I was still fairly anonymous; it was basically only the people who knew about sport who recognised me. That has obviously changed now. I find it very nice and flattering in one way being recognised. Sometimes you meet people and they are so thrilled by what you have done. I met one woman after the Olympics, and her eyes filled up with tears. She had to walk away because she had become so emotional, and that was very touching. I never realised, while I was in Atlanta, the effect it was having on people here. Sometimes, though, it gets to be too much, and I need my privacy. I still want to keep to as normal a life as I can.

'It is very hard for me to come to grips with my achievement at the moment. It was not something I expected to do going out there. I did have great expectations of a medal, but I knew that in order for me to achieve that, it would entail an enormous amount of hard work. In the months building up to it, I cut everything out; and by the end of January, I had isolated myself for my preparation. We just did the same things that we normally did minus the PR work. That kind of work had meant getting a flight to Ireland and losing a training day and a rest day. So even if I had gone to do a day's work in Ireland, I would have lost out on at least three days' training because I would have been so tired when I got back, having missed my rest.'

Erik agrees. 'There was no point drawing up a programme then allowing somebody else to shoot holes in it, because then there would be no balance. If you take one element out, it is very hard to make up for the time lost.'

To appreciate the dedication that walked hand in hand with Erik and Michelle *en route* to Atlanta, it is necessary only to examine her training schedule last Christmas. Throughout the festive season, Michelle kept to her training programme. Even when Christmas Day itself dawned in Dordrecht, she and Erik headed down to the local pool mid-afternoon to conduct their ritual training session –

Christmas day or no Christmas day. Unfortunately they had no permission to open the building; and when they did so, they triggered an alarm system without knowing it themselves. The president of the club got up from his Christmas dinner to rush down to the pool, fearing theft. The caretaker of the pool left his table and hot-footed it to the pool.

And all the time Michelle trained on, oblivious to the fuss around her. The caretaker didn't take kindly to the fact that she had trained on as all hell broke loose around her. He reported Michelle and Erik to the council who owned the pool.

Michelle continued to train hard after Christmas. She clocked up 200 kilometres a week in the pool. She lifted weights in the new gym beside her home in Holland. She put up with the sneers as she hopped her way like a frog around that gym, building up her muscles and her stamina, building the swimmer that would defy the critics and the cynics in such a devastating fashion. When people asked her about the effectiveness of her slick tumble turns in Atlanta, she had only to refer them back to the hours leaping like a frog in a Dutch gymnasium when those around her first laughed, then questioned her sanity.

Most swimmers like to taper their training, to ease down their preparations a couple of weeks before a big event and save themselves to peak in the big race. Michelle Smith did not adhere to that tradition. As a result of her performances at the Olympics many swimmers will now ditch that regime.

Michelle explains, 'We had a very specific programme worked out and we stuck to it rigidly. It was based around my fitness and weights work in the gym, and my speed and stamina work in the pool. It was a carefully planned, carefully plotted schedule. I had a list of things to do each week, and I had to stick to those lists if I wanted to achieve success at the Olympics. I had to be better than in Vienna to win. That meant the training had to be better as well. It was.

'Race wise, I went to Toulouse in France in March and I did quite well there considering that I hadn't rested that much prior to the meet or done much preparation. My times were quite good, better than the times I had done a month or five weeks prior to the European Championships. Before that Toulouse competition we had been doing a lot more long-distance work than we had done before the Europeans, so I did have a heavy programme in France. But even at the end of that weekend, I felt I had a very good level of fitness although the speed wasn't there yet. That wasn't a concern; I didn't have to be fast at that stage.

'In Toulouse I won the 200-metre individual medley and was second in the 200-metre butterfly. I literally cannot remember any of the other races; but I wasn't there for spectacular times, just to get an idea of where I stood regarding fitness and preparation for Atlanta.'

It got serious in April. 'About six weeks before the Olympics I said to my manager, Kathy Stapleton, to say "no" to any requests for interviews. It was time to concentrate just on training. I wanted to have those last few weeks to think solely of my training and not to have people asking me if I thought I was going to win a medal. The more times you hear that, the more pressure it puts on you. Whenever I am in Ireland, I try to accommodate whatever reporters I can; but when I am in my training regime in Holland, I don't want people coming over and upsetting that.

'After that, the next big competition I entered was the Dutch National Championships in the summer. I did well there, particularly in the 200-metre freestyle when I brought the Irish record down from 2:04 to 2:00 flat. That was my best time by quite a few seconds. It wasn't my record I broke; it had been set by my Olympic team-mate Marion Madine.

'I was getting a little bit more speed by that stage and I knew that my general fitness was at a good level. After that, Erik said to me that I was ready to do a really good 400-metre freestyle. So, from that point on, we were looking for a competition where I could do a 400-metre freestyle just to see what I could do.'

Curiosity was growing in the swimming pools of Europe. The opponents who had suffered in Michelle Smith's slipstream in Vienna were beginning to wonder where they stood vis à vis the Irish girl in the weeks before Atlanta. She left them waiting – and guessing.

Michelle saw the situation like this: 'A lot of swimmers would have two occasions during the year where they would taper, which is when they cut down in training and increase their rest to keep themselves tuned up for a certain competition where they want to do really well. Most swimmers would do that for one competition between January and March, so a lot of them were asking me during the year where exactly it was that I was going to swim fast pre-Atlanta.

'I didn't really swim anywhere – deliberately. I just kept the training going, and that was part of the overall scheme as well. I had no problem with the people I had swum against in Europe knowing I was going to be in good shape in Atlanta – but they couldn't know how good. So that was part of the game as well: keeping the competition guessing.

'The next swim outside training was in a small competition in Holland when I did a good 100-metre breaststroke in 1:10, less than a tenth of a second outside the Irish record and an improvement on my personal best of four seconds. That was a good indication for me that my breaststroke was going well for the individual medley as that had always been my weakest stroke.

'Then the Dutch Championships were held in Drachten, and I became entangled in another bit of controversy. I didn't actually win the 200-metre freestyle there. They have a rule in swimming competitions that you can swim a heat in the morning and you have thirty minutes after the announcement of the final to pull out of it. That's the norm across the world, but they have a rule in Holland for the Dutch National Championships that says you cannot do that. You have to let them know when you are putting in your entry that you do not want to swim the final. So I was swimming a 200-metre freestyle event in the morning and after that, I think, it was a 100-metre butterfly.

'I wanted to try to swim a fast 100-metre butterfly in the evening, so the ideal thing for me was to withdraw from the final of the freestyle and just swim the butterfly, partly because the freestyle was before the butterfly and there was less than five minutes between the two races. But I wasn't allowed to withdraw so I just got into the final of the freestyle and swam it really slowly, which just wasn't appreciated, particularly when I swam the 100-metre butterfly fast minutes later and won. The officials took offence and disqualified me from the 200-metre freestyle for swimming too slowly. That's almost unheard of in swimming; it doesn't matter how slowly you swim.

'So I left for Atlanta as the Dutch 100-metre butterfly champion and 400-metre individual medley champion too, where my time was 4:52 which was comparable with what I had been doing prior to the Europeans. If anything, I was in much better condition than I had been when I swam the Irish Nationals in 1995 prior to Vienna.'

Michelle Smith's departure for Atlanta went unnoticed by the press. The rest of the Irish team flew out of Dublin one Monday morning to a fanfare of trumpets. Michelle and Erik also flew out of Dublin that morning. They chekced in early though and avoided all the fuss, slipping into the departure area without anyone noticing them. They escaped the cameras and the media. It was the quiet exit they wanted en route to Florida and the training camp where acclimatisation to heat and humidity would prove so crucial.

As Michelle says, 'It was important to get to America early and acclimatise. Atlanta's weather was to become one of the big talking points during the Olympics. The temperatures there are right up at the end of July so it was vital to sample that heat and humidity as early as possible and vital to get accustomed to it.

'In Florida, we were in a place near Fort Lauderdale for training camp, half an hour south of Miami. When we arrived, we found that our training times had not been organised as we would have wished and it caused problems. We had pool time from 12 noon to 2 p.m. and from 8 p.m. until 10 p.m. which is totally out of synch with my normal training. We tried to change it; but we couldn't get a lane, so we went looking for an alternative. The head coach at Fort Lauderdale had a group swimming in five or six lanes with mostly one or two swimmers per lane. Normally you can have up to six swimmers in a lane in a 50-metre pool and swimming comfortably, so we asked if he could accommodate us. He just wouldn't co-operate; he wouldn't let me into any one of those lanes.

'That left us with no option but to organise pool time elsewhere. Eventually we got an offer to train in a pool called Pine Crest thanks to the intervention of Sam Freas, president of swimming's International Hall of Fame. Pine Crest was ideal for my pre-Olympic training, with a private pool whose only users were the kids at summer camps. They just ignored me and let me get on with my Olympic build-up in one of the lanes in the 50-metre pool. It was a relief because even the coach at the club in Fort Lauderdale where I had trained before had refused to help when I went looking for assistance after our early problems in Florida.

'For the duration of the three-week training camp we stayed with the rest of the Irish team who had travelled out to Lynn University, a college with connections in Ireland that had offered our Olympic Council their facilities for anyone who wanted to set up training camp pre-Atlanta. The boxers, cyclists, tennis players and swimmers took them up on the offer. And once again it was the boxers who struck up an immediate rapport.

'The main problem I had with the original pool on offer was the heat of the afternoon sun when they wanted us to train from 12 noon to 2 p.m. The second time booked every day was from 8 p.m. to 10 p.m. – but I'm normally well asleep by 9 p.m. after my evening stint in the pool. Had we taken those times, I wouldn't have been back at base, fed and in bed before midnight. We never even tried it.

'Pine Crest was a totally different kettle of fish. The summer camp kids trained twice a day. The rest of the time the facility, made available solely to me, was there for us.'

Erik agreed: 'One of the nice things there was that we could train when we wanted.' And Michelle continued: 'I had the whole pool to myself, an eight-lane 50-metre pool with only Erik on the bank, so that was a luxury. It was so nice compared to Fort Lauderdale where there were other teams training in the pool and it was so busy. That first pool was also open to the public but the Italian and Venezuelan Olympic squads and a group of Belgian junior swimmers were there on camps as well. On one of the few occasions we trained there, the Italians had just arrived, and every single move I made was put under scrutiny by the coaches and then the swimmers. It was nice to get away from the prying eyes and to have some privacy to ourselves at Pine Crest.

'We were there for quite some time, arriving on 26 June and leaving on 18 July. It was totally focused: we trained, we rested, we ate, and we swam. We didn't even have time for sightseeing bar two hours one day looking around the swamps. We were both very conscious at that stage that we were in the last stage of preparation and it was most important to get maximum training and rest in-between. The last thing we wanted was to train hard and then to run around sightseeing. That would have constituted a waste of energy. So we didn't get to see the alligators!

'It was all part of an Olympic master plan. Everything had to be right for Atlanta. Thankfully the people at the college we stayed at were exceptionally good. The food was great there which was important. And they were very accommodating. They normally finished dinner around 7 p.m. but we didn't finish training until 8 p.m. We couldn't get into the cafeteria until 8.45 p.m., but they used to keep the cook back especially to look after us and to make sure there was a hot meal ready for us.

'There was not that much expectation of the Irish team at this stage. I don't think, until I did the 400-metre freestyle, that people expected anything of me. Besides, everyone was getting ready for his or her own event. As in Seoul and Barcelona, the boxers were the best craic, and Francie Barrett was the best of them all. He was a real character, a real charmer with the appetite of two men. Francie was also so proud to be fighting for Ireland in Atlanta – and we were so proud of him.

'My interest in boxing goes back to 1988 when I met Michael Carruth and Wayne McCullough for the first time in Seoul. Every time after that, whenever I was home in the summer, I'd go down to the National Stadium, and my dad and I would talk to Wayne and his coach and trade stories about training and the lack of funds and how hard it was! I remember being very impressed by Wayne at the Olympics in 1988. He was somebody who stood out from the rest of the team. His dedication was like that of a swimmer's.

'When the two of them, Wayne and Michael, won their medals, I said to my dad that next time Wayne was going to go on to be a world champion. He always had that commitment in him. I'm delighted that I've been proven right. When the others were taking it easy, he was out there training, going for a run, working his body. He was the most dedicated of them all – he trained like a maniac. He has what it takes. I saw him on TV recently and wanted to go and see one of his professional fights in Dublin; but I was in Holland and so I couldn't make it. I spoke to him on the phone when I was in Atlanta; he and his wife were sitting in Vegas watching it on TV, jumping up and down.'

All that was another day's work. For now Michelle and Erik needed a race to test her 400-metre freestyle times in. That race came at her pre-Atlanta training camp in Pine Crest, at an invitational meet where Michelle Smith raced nobody but herself.

As Michelle recalls, 'The 400-metre individual freestyle competition was going to be held in Pine Crest where I was training. I asked them if I could enter and they agreed. We did not know beforehand that this was going to be on.'

Erik continued, 'I had asked around for competitions while we were there and it transpired that the one that was the nearest to us was right on our doorstep.'

'But,' says Michelle, 'there were no other competitors in the race. I was on my own. There was nobody else in the pool. They were all junior swimmers, kids at camp, and they didn't want to pit them against me, so they had a special heat for me where I raced alone. It was the same as a normal race with official timekeepers, but we had signals where Erik would let me know during the race how I was doing.

'When you swim freestyle, you are looking to the right and the left alternately so you can see somebody at the side of the pool. We had these signals pre-arranged that Erik would point in different directions depending on what I was to do, this way for faster, and thumbs up if I was on pace. So those were the signals that I would be watching for during the first 200 metres, as it is in the first 200 metres that you really need to get your pace right.

'If you go out too fast, you might blow it on the last 100 metres. If you go out too slowly, you can forget it as you will never make it up. I ended up with the fastest time in the world so far this year, and second fastest of all the qualifiers for the Olympics. It was faster than we had anticipated; neither of us thought I would get under 4:10. I thought I might have been able to make 4:14 or around that because I was just starting into my taper for the Olympics, and I was not fully rested. The fact that I made 4:08 was an incredible bonus.

'The American coach who ran the training camps, two Australian coaches who were helping out, and an Irish girl called Leanne, who was out there coaching, were all thrilled for me when the time went up. There was a great sense of excitement afterwards. Everyone was delighted. Jay Fitzgerald, the man who ran the pool and all the summer camps, had put quite a few people on American swimming teams himself and he was ecstatic. He knew exactly what the time meant.

'On the day of the race, his leg was in plaster and he was on crutches at the side of the pool, watching my 400-metre freestyle. Erik got really excited at the end of the freestyle, and he was so delighted that he went over to Jay, put his hand up to give him a high five, and nearly put Jay backwards on his bad leg, almost breaking the other one!'

Erik chuckled. 'Afterwards we were sitting in his house with his wife and he said, "Gee, I was afraid you would break my other leg!" He is not Irish but he is of Irish descent. His wife's name is Murphy, and his name is Fitzgerald.'

Michelle continued the story. 'Getting that time in the race meant so much and it was then that I decided I wanted to compete in the 400-metre freestyle in the Olympics. I went to the Irish Olympic coach, Bobby Madine, Marion's father, who was there as well, and I told him that, after doing my new time, I wanted to swim the event on two provisions. His daughter had been entered for that event but she only had a "B" qualifying time, and in order for two swimmers to swim the event, both would have to have the "A" qualifying time. If I were to swim the event, she would not have been able to. I said I'd pull out of two of my other events, the 200-metre freestyle and 100-metre butterfly, which were more her events anyway. I let her swim those events, and she pulled out of the 400-metre freestyle. It was just a matter of changing names. This all happened on the sixth. Then FINA, the world swimming regulators, came back and said the deadline had been the fifth.

'When I had spoken to Bobby in Pine Crest about the time and the changing of the entries, he said that he had the manual upstairs, so we read through it ourselves. It said that one could make changes and corrections up until 17 July, so we thought that everything would be fine. It was not really a new entry anyway; it was just a change of competitors. There would have been a problem if Ireland had had no entry in the event, but we did have one. All we wanted to do was to change the name. Within the guidelines laid out in that manual, we had another ten days to do that. Everything we did then was within the law, the law written down in their guidebook.

'The Irish team went to Atlanta on the 15th and that was the first provisional meeting for handing in your entries, with the actual deadline on the 17th. Then, when we actually got to Atlanta, the Olympic Council said that we had until the 20th to change the entry for the 400-metre freestyle, but it should have been the 18th. It was only then that we realised that FINA were not going to accept it because they were sticking to the date of the 5th, even though the manual said one could make changes and corrections up to the 17th.

'As it turned out, however, I had swum the 400-metre freestyle within the qualifying time last year, so I could have taken another qualifying time as well. I had that option. That is what a lot of the American papers didn't print, that I already had a qualifying time for that event one year and three months prior to the Olympics. But the problem wasn't about the qualifying time; the problem was about when the entry was put in. Then, because the Olympic Council of Ireland was able to produce the manual which they had issued us with – and because it was down on paper – they had to admit that they had made a mistake and stand by the rules of the manual.'

The final piece of the jigsaw was almost in place. Michelle Smith had her time for the 400-metre freestyle. She had the fastest time in the world that year to boot. She was ready to make the move: to Georgia; to Atlanta; to the land of golden dreams.

CHAPTER ELEVEN

Atlanta Diary

THURSDAY, 18 JULY

The Irish Olympic team arrived in Atlanta on 15 July – without Michelle Smith. She had decided to stay back an extra three nights in Florida to begin her taper at the Pine Crest pool, and to stay away from the cauldron of emotion and excitement that was part and parcel of the Olympic village. This would allow her to wind down her preparations in isolation, with only Erik to help her focus on the four events to come. It would also allow her to escape the media frenzy that had been surrounding her entry for the 400-metre freestyle. And it allowed Michelle and Erik to miss the endless queues for accreditation that had greeted the Irish team on their earlier arrival.

Michelle and Erik take up the story. 'Because we arrived later than all the national squads when we flew from Miami to Atlanta, the rigmarole of getting accredited didn't take too long,' says Michelle. 'I just didn't want to get into the village on the 15th, so for the last three days we were on our own in Florida. That worked in our favour when it came to accreditation for both myself and Erik.'

'There was never any problem with my coach's accreditation,' says Eric. 'I had heard stories from Ireland that I would have a problem but that was nonsense. I applied via the Olympic Council of Ireland through the normal channels and that was that.'

Michelle says: 'Erik was accredited as my coach. I'm a firm believer in one coach, one swimmer. It has worked for me, and I am sure it will be the way forward for top-class swimmers in the future. Erik has had problems with accreditation in the past, notably in Rome for the World Championships, but there was no problem in Atlanta.

'The Irish swimming team did have their own coach there, Bobby

Madine, but we had no tactical contact with him. We always work by ourselves, just the two of us. I think they are used to us by now. Last year, in Vienna, we were considered the rebels because we did our own thing; but I'm not prepared to compromise or change. I have my own way of preparing with Erik that has always worked for me in the past. Maybe because I do things differently from the rest of the swimming team, I am considered an outsider. I can live with that.

'However, I do socialise with the other swimmers, particularly Earl McCarthy. Because he lives and trains in Germany, he thinks a little bit differently from the others too. He has a wider view of the international scene and what is needed to compete, something that is sadly missing in Irish swimming.'

One of the first things Michelle Smith did on her arrival in Atlanta was to check out the Olympic pool at the Georgia Tech.

Michelle continues: 'Swimmers are like every other sports people: we have our superstitions and our little quirks. We like to know the feel of the pool we're about to compete in, the height of the starting blocks, even the pattern on the roof tiles which is so important during the backstroke. I was happy enough with the pool in Atlanta when I went into the Georgia water for the first time on the day I arrived.

'It was relatively easy for us on the Thursday before the games began to get into the Olympic village, get ourselves sorted in our accommodation, get accredited and then get down to the pool for a short swim and a look around just 48 hours before the start of competition.

'Normally the Olympic pool is open air, but not in Atlanta. For all the teams, the heat, the humidity and the blazing sun presented problems for the swimmers, so the organising committee extended a temporary roof over the pool to take the glare of the afternoon sun out of our eyes. I hadn't come across a temporary roof like that before, so it was important to check it out. Believe me, the wrong design on a roof, the wrong tile on the ceiling, the wrong reflection off the sun can make all the difference. There's one 50-metre pool in England, for example, that we all hate going to swim in because of the design of the tiles in the roof. When you're swimming the backstroke they can be really off-putting.

'You also need to check little things like the backstroke flags positioned over the pool so that you know exactly when to prepare to turn on the different legs of the distance events. It is a bit of a ritual to check the flags, the roof, even the height of the starting blocks for the moment you want to push off and hit the water. Remember that in Barcelona, four years earlier, for example, Gary O'Toole was off balance when they started the heat for the 200-metre breaststroke, his first event at that games. He never recovered from that bad start.'

That explains why visitors to the Olympic pool that Thursday would have seen the girl from Ireland practising her backstroke and counting flags.

'I just did half an hour or so in the pool on the Thursday. At that stage, I was tapering for the race on Saturday, but it was vital to have a look at the pool and get a feel for it.'

Erik explains: 'It is normal practice for a big meet, a case of getting used to the pool as it is the first time you have seen it, the first time you will be swimming in it. You want to see how high the blocks are, feel the temperature of the water, see where the flags are for your backstroke, how the sides of the pool are . . . small things – but important things – that ensure you don't just come in on the day of your competition and find something off-putting like the height of the starting blocks.'

Michelle adds, 'Little things can cause big problems. A swimmer may not have noticed lights high up on the ceiling before the race that can shine into his or her eyes and blind him or her temporarily. That sort of thing can cost a swimmer a race come competition time.'

'It is also important to get a feel for the poolside environment, to check out the warm-up pool, the tunnel area, and the call-room where the swimmers go just before their heats and their finals,' explains Erik.

Michelle continues: 'It is important to know your way around from the training pool where you warm up before you enter the main arena for competition. There is a call-room outside the Olympic pool where they check off your name; you have to be there three heats, or 15 minutes, before your event. But, in Atlanta, it was a little more relaxed; so I would check my name in, go back to the tunnel area and then come in at the very last minute. There is a lot of psyching out in the call-room. When you win a medal, you walk in there for the next race with your head held high. Your attitude and your demeanour in the call-room can act as a secret weapon. Erik used to play these mind games when he was a competitor and he taught me to do the same. I would wait until the last minute to go into the call-room, then walk in and let all the other girls watch me without looking at anyone. While they were working out what sort of form I was in, I would start swinging, stretching and preparing. Most of them would sit down, but I would remain standing, letting them know that I was ready for victory. Four years ago, I would not have done that. I'd have sat there as meek as a lamb.'

Michelle used that Thursday session at the Olympic pool to acclimatise to the new surroundings, and to come to terms with the fever pitch that had accompanied the swimming agenda of the 1996 games.

'I knew going to the Atlanta Olympics, that swimming was going to be one of the really big events. They have always had one or two stars in US swimming so it is a popular sport. That led to a massive demand for tickets. There were only 15,000 seats in there, so it was one of the smallest Olympic venues there in terms of capacity. The Olympic Council told us that boxing and swimming were the hardest events to get tickets for. If they had had 20,000 or 25,000 tickets they'd have sold them all.

'Even as a competitor, I got no tickets . . . not even for Erik. If there are tickets left over, the coaches are allowed into the stands – but only if there are seats empty. Otherwise, they have to watch in the tunnel area, below the pool. Once or twice, Erik did get such a seat in Atlanta but those seats were scarce. My manager, Kathy Stapleton, had to pay $250 on the black market more than once to get a ticket – and a ticket is valid for just one morning or one evening session. It is not valid for the day. Thankfully, my family knew months in advance that the tickets were going to be in hot demand so they made early arrangements with the Olympic Council.

'Aside from the ticket issue, I made a point of not thinking about the crowd, the size of it, or who was in it. I remembered freezing on the blocks in Barcelona, and I didn't want to do that again. I didn't want to be overwhelmed by swimming in front of so many people. Normally I swim in front of 150 to 200 people. The prospect of having 15,000 people screaming at you – and the majority of them American – was not something I thought about – deliberately. I decided after that first visit to the pool to ignore the crowd and concentrate on my race: to just look into the pool, down my lane, and to think about my race and my tactics, and what I wanted to do.'

All that was to come two days later. For now, Michelle and Erik had new quarters to settle into. The Olympic village does not suit all Olympians. Some choose to stay away from the centre of attention and attraction and closet themselves in hotels. Others rent luxury houses and pamper themselves in the build-up to their events. Michelle Smith had an option on all such luxuries. She opted to stay with her Irish team-mates in the village.

'It was important for me to be a part of the team, and also important to stay with the team in the village. But I can understand why the likes of Sonia O'Sullivan opted to stay outside. She felt it was the best preparation for her and I respect that decision. There was a lot of pressure on Sonia going into the games. Being away from the village would have eased her exposure to that pressure. Sonia isolated herself before and during the games, staying away from the block.

'I also had that option; but, for me, the pool was practically in the village, right across from the cafeteria. We had thought about staying away as it was that much noisier in the village. If I had stayed in a hotel it would have taken over an hour in the morning just to get to the pool. The amount of travelling to the pool for practice, returning to the hotel and then there and back for the heats and finals again would have taken four hours in the day. I simply could not afford the time with four events in six days, so we decided to stay in the village at the beginning and see how it would work out.'

All was not well though on the accommodation front. Sonia O'Sullivan's decision to stay away from the athletes' village seemed a wise one when Michelle checked her room out.

'We had one of the worst rooms I had ever seen,' recalls Michelle. 'We had no pillows, and the sheets were only just about clean. They were changed once while we were there. The blinds didn't work so we had to tape newspapers on the windows. I had to ask for a bin six times before I eventually got one, and then, two days later, they came in and took it away, so I nearly had a fit. Even the air-conditioning didn't work so I had to ask Shay McDonald, the *chef de mission*, to buy me a cooling fan downtown. Thankfully he did.

'It sounds like I was looking for the Hilton but I wasn't. I just needed some comfort – some peace and some quiet to concentrate on my competitions for the first nine days that I was there. After that it wouldn't have mattered; then we could have been part of the crazy hustle and bustle that is part and parcel of an Olympic village.

'But, unfortunately, that's always the way: in Atlanta, the first few days in the village were very noisy so I ended up going to another block to rest between the heats and the finals. Erik's sister, Corrie, was over in the Dutch block; and there was only one athlete and the team manager there in her apartment. Their accommodation was like a hotel compared with ours, which was more like a dormitory. I don't know how it happened but it was really noisy; every time somebody opened or closed a door in the corridor you could hear it all over the building. And when people were walking down the corridor you could hear them talking. I think it was just the way things worked out with countries being allocated their accommodation. The block the Dutch were in was newly built, but the Irish appeared to have got the student accommodation. I think it had been a fraternity block before we got there. It went back to being a fraternity house as soon as the Irish team left.'

When Michelle arrived, she was the subject of media attention almost immediately. There were two topics of conversation that first day. One was the chance of Ireland's female stars, Sonia and Michelle, bringing home gold. The other was the thorny subject of the 400-metre freestyle.

'I knew there were a lot of requests for interviews that Thursday to discuss both subjects but I had to keep a low profile; I had to remain focused on Saturday's 400-metre individual medley,' says Michelle. 'Naturally I had expected that Sonia would be in the spotlight for the games. I had also expected people to say that the focus at these games was going to be on the two women – that Sonia and I were going to have to win the medals for Ireland.

'I didn't like that idea. I always felt that since on paper I was never in the top five in any of my events going into the games, in black and white terms, I was not going to be somebody they could classify in the top three and say that I had a great chance. I might have been in the top eight, but certainly not the top three. Whereas Sonia was; she was winning all around her. She was the world champion; and if you were a betting person, you would have bet your house that she was going to win the 5,000 metres.

'I watched the 5,000-metre race in the Irish block with a lot of the other athletes. I think there was complete silence when she ran off the track because nobody knew what was wrong with her. At first we didn't know if she was sick or not. We were trying to see if she was limping off the track in case she had been spiked. Then, the next day, she sent a fax to all the athletes saying that she was okay and that she had no major problems; so we never did know what was wrong with her.'

There was also the thorny issue of the 400-metre freestyle entry, a debate that was running and running in the Irish media, a debate that was beginning to arouse interest Stateside. Michelle could not afford to get involved.

'Because we deliberately landed in Atlanta just two days before my first event, we went straight into this hornets' nest about the 400-metre freestyle entry. I ignored it all when I arrived in the Olympic village and let the capable Pat Hickey and his OCI committee get on with it. I had to. I just couldn't afford to divert any attention away from the 400-metre individual medley on the Saturday.

'Before we left Florida, after the fast time at Pine Crest, we were very anxious to get things sorted out, to have the entry in before we got there. By the time we got to Atlanta, it was still up in the air; but I had to forget all about it, calm down and ensure that I didn't waste energy getting upset about it. In fact, Erik told me to forget about the 400-metre freestyle, and whether I could swim it or not, and just to concentrate on the first race. If all that furore had happened four years earlier in my swimming career, it probably would have devastated me.

'Looking back on it now, I don't know if it was FINA or the organising committee in Atlanta who was the guilty party. Certainly, the organising committee sent out the wrong information in a booklet. One of their men, who had spoken to the Olympic Council, came out at one of the meetings and admitted that he had given the OCI false information. We had asked for the entry to be confirmed on 7 July after the Pine Crest time, which was well within the deadline given to the Irish delegation.'

The entry for the 400-metre freestyle was to become a thorny issue. There were, though, some lighter moments for Erik and Michelle in the early days of the Centennial games. Michelle Smith was one of the athletes allocated a golf cart to get around the village in the run-up to her main events. It was repeatedly stolen and hot-wired by entrepreneurial types around the village. Erik had to explain that one to the Irish *chef de mission* Shay McDonald a few times. He also had a run-in with an Olympic traffic warden of all things.

Michelle takes up the story: 'Every team was allocated a golf cart; it was allocated to the *chef de mission*, but, on the days we were competing, I was given the keys. If you were relying on the transport in the village, it could take you twenty minutes to get to the pool; whereas, in the golf cart, it would take you little more than five. So when we had our own transport, we just left it outside the pool; and when we were finished training or racing, we got ourselves to the cafeteria and back in ten or 15 minutes instead of the 45 minutes on the infamous Olympic transport system. Erik drove, but he drove a little too fast at times – so fast that we got stopped by the Olympic police!'

'They had these people in uniform and they thought they were really important,' adds Erik.

'One guy had a problem with us,' continues Michelle. 'It had started to get dark and Erik thought the guy was saying, "Put your lights on." He waved and turned his lights on. The guy came back and stopped us. He thought Erik was being smart. He had told Erik to slow down. Erik had shouted back that he'd put his lights on. The guy thought he was saying: "Pull my licence" – which could have been misconstrued.'

There was also a decision to be made on swimwear that first day in Atlanta. Michelle had, like the rest of the swimming team, been given the go-ahead to wear Speedo, the IASA sponsors, inside the pool if she so wished. Outside she had to wear training gear with the Reebok label, the Olympic sponsor. She was going to wear the revolutionary long aquablade suit she had worn for that brilliant 400-metre freestyle swim in Pine Crest.

'I had tried out this new aquablade suit two months before the Olympics. I was pretty sceptical about it being revolutionary because I don't believe everything I am told. But I had tried it, and felt that it was a good swimsuit. The idea behind it is that the material has less resistance than your skin, so the logical conclusion is that the more skin it covers the faster you will be.

'I felt that if it could make the difference of one one-hundredth or one two-hundredth of a second, then it could be the difference between winning and losing a medal. So, why not use something that can make that difference?

'First impressions count. There was certainly less resistance when I used the longer suit at the Dutch nationals for the first time prior to flying out to America. And it swung it for me when I used the suit for that 400-metre freestyle time three weeks before the games. I had a load of them; but although I am not one for superstition, I wore the same green suit that I had worn in the 400-metre freestyle in Pine Crest for all my finals. Normally I would change them, but not in Atlanta. It was my lucky omen – and it worked.

'At the moment, the gold-medal suit is in Holland, but I don't think I'll frame it. We're not given to hanging mementoes on the wall. Not yet, anyway.'

Atlanta Diary

FRIDAY, 19 JULY

They opened the Olympics on this day, 1996. They opened the games with pomp and ceremony. They opened with an extravaganza as only America can do. They kept the greatest secret until last. Mohammed Ali was the man to light the Olympic flame in Atlanta's very own field of dreams. 'The Greatest' brought the house down as he took the torch from the American swimmer, Janet Evans, and fuelled dreams and flames in one swift movement.

Michelle Smith watched Mohammed Ali from the comfort of her pew in the Irish quarters at the Olympic village. She watched with pride as the boxer, Francie Barrett, carried the tricolour into the stadium, just as she had done in Barcelona four years earlier. She watched from the comfort of an armchair because tomorrow was D-day, judgement day. As ever, the swimming was to begin the morning after the night before, the night of the opening ceremony.

For Michelle and the rest of the Irish swimming team, Friday was the last day of preparation: the last chance to check the Olympic pool – the turns, the light, the glare of the morning sun, the flags to signal the approaching wall in the backstroke. Friday was the last day to check the formalities, a day to think of competition and opposition.

The first thing that struck Michelle Smith when she trained in Atlanta was the sheer size of the Olympic swimming stadium. It was massive: a big arena with a crowd capacity in the region of 15,000, the biggest venue she'd ever swum in. The 1991 World Championships in Perth had seated about 10,000 to 12,000 spectators; the 1988 Olympics in Seoul seated even less.

Because it was America, there was also a big demand for the

swimming tickets – a record demand. The undesirable scalpers – 'touts' on this side of the world – had a field day. The American public like their swimming; they have a history and tradition in the sport that upped the ante for the scalpers, and raised the price for the fans – Irish, American or any other race or creed.

Swimming was one of the hottest events in a hot town on the back of one good fact: the Americans like the sport. Talk to your average American sports fan about it and he or she will quickly point to the achievements of Mark Spitz and Janet Evans, great athletes and great Olympians in their time. For American patriots, the power of sport is almost as awesome as the power of the dollar. The Yank fans and media alike love their swimming because it has traditionally served up Olympic medals on a plate for them. Their public and their media wanted to be at the poolside when Janet Evans, Alison Wagner and Brooke Bennett, their 16-year-old long-distance sensation, picked up gold medal after gold medal. That was the script.

If only Michelle Smith had read the script beforehand, a script that was plain for all to see. Janet Evans, triple gold medal winner at the tender age of 17 in Seoul and the winner of gold and silver medals four years later in Barcelona, talked a great race before she stubbed her pretty little toes in the Georgian waters.

Evans was the quintessential American hero. At 17, she went to the 1988 Olympic games and dominated the swimming events with a stroke so unorthodox that one American writer likened it to a wind-up bathtub toy. In two of her events, the 400-metre and 800-metre freestyle, Evans set world records. The girl from Placentia, California, described it, pre-Atlanta, as 'a fairytale come true'. But Evans also claimed that she lost her identity when she found those gold medals and that world-class form at the Seoul games. Plain 'Janet' had now become known as 'Janet, the Olympic Champion'.

By the advent of the '92 games in Barcelona, Evans had grown four inches and put on a stone. Janet Evans was no longer the wind-up bathtub toy. She lost her 400-metre freestyle title to Dagmar Hase of Germany in the last 50 metres, losing by 0.19 of a second and barely recognising the silver medal as a consolation. Her first loss over the distance in six years produced tears at the post-race press conference. America's hero was losing grip of her halo and her paddle.

Still, she regained them after much cajoling from her parents and coach, Mark Schubert, in time for the 800-metre freestyle when she took the fourth gold medal of her short 21-year lifespan.

All was not well though: Janet Evans did not see the bottom of a pool for four months after Barcelona. When she was invited to public functions to display her gold medals, she would bring only the three from Korea. The fourth, from Barcelona, was the blacksheep of her medal family; it was there – somewhere – but never seen in public.

With a hint of the reaction to come from this falling star of American sport, she described her emotions after that Spanish collapse. 'I'd been trying to live up to my past and it was impossible,' Evans told *USA Today*. 'It was just impossible. I was so into setting world records that I wasn't used to finishing second or third. It was hard for me. When I failed in the pool I felt like a failure as a person. Swimming ate me up inside.'

Janet Evans made it clear before she touched a drop of water in the Olympic pool in Atlanta that she was going to quit after her last race and, she assumed, her last medal, in July of 1996. She was going to spend more time on a personal appearance circuit that had already grossed her a six-figure Olympic-size salary for endorsements and speeches. All she needed in Atlanta was one more gold medal to equal the speed skater Bonnie Blair's collection of five golds.

The Atlanta games were special to Evans for other reasons. She had been a part of the city's successful bid to land the games, accompanying chief executive officer Billy Payne to Tokyo when their bid – their dream – came true. And on the night of the opening ceremony, she was the last person before Mohammed Ali to hold the Olympic torch on its way to the cauldron. The greatest swimmer met 'The Greatest'.

The fact that Evans had only finished fifth in the 400-metre freestyle at the 1994 World Championships in Rome, where she had won the 800-metre freestyle, did not bother the great American public. Janet Evans, holder of three world records, three American records and a degree in communications, was going to win gold and join Bonnie Blair in the hall of the immortals at the Atlanta games. That was the weight of expectation Michelle Smith was racing against in the 400-metre freestyle – not just against the legendary Evans.

Michelle Smith noticed Janet Evans's presence on the screen that opening night. She only just noticed it; nothing more and nothing less. She had a race the next day. She had a heat to qualify in. She had a medal to win.

'The day before my first race, I did my training session and I had my rest. I made a very deliberate effort not to get caught up in the Olympic spirit because I had learnt . . . both from my own mistakes in the European Championships, World Championships and previous Olympics and from the mistakes of others that I had witnessed and studied over the years. I knew how the Olympics could affect people in terms of pressure and hype, and I didn't want to let that get to me. I remember watching one of the guys I had swum with in Calgary, the Canadian, Mark Tewksbury, at the Barcelona games. He had been the third best backstroker in the world for two or three years, but there were two Americans he could just never beat. One of those was Jeff Rouse, the American champion and the world record holder. He was a certainty for the gold; but, in the final, the Americans spent all their time watching each other and worrying about each other, so much so that Mark came through and pipped them both to the gold medal. To rub it in even more, when Rouse went on to swim the medley relay, he swam the backstroke leg so fast that he smashed the world record. But it was too late.

'I knew how this unique Olympic pressure affected people, how you can win and lose races that way. I went back to experience. I tried to think of the Olympics as being just the same as the European Championships. I had to dismiss any suggestion that this was a situation where the expectation levels of others in my ability could weigh me down. I had to look back to Vienna, to my European Championship gold medals and be positive.'

Michelle Smith knew the night before her first competition that this was destined to be her first real Olympic challenge. In 1988, she had been too young to be a force against the best the world had to offer. In 1992, she had been injured and was ill prepared. But now, in 1996, she was dedicated to swimming with a coach who had revolutionised her training, her life and her career. At this moment, Michelle Smith knew why swimming meant so much to her, as she explains.

'In terms of sport, swimming stands out for me – and not just because I like the water. As an individual, your results are solely dependent on whatever training you put in. You are responsible for the performance and the result. But in a team sport, you can be as good as the best player or as bad as the worst.

'The other thing I like is the structure of the race. You get up on the blocks; you dive off; you swim your race; you touch the wall; and your time comes up on the electronic scoreboard. That's it. It is there for all to see. There is no debate, no mark for artistic merit. It is a race to the line. Nobody sits in judgement like they do in boxing or ice-skating.

'In swimming, whatever you do, you do yourself. You swim your own race. At the end of the race, nobody can dispute the time or the result.'

The night before the start of competition is worry time for the average athlete: worry about the preparations, the plans, the tactics. That is, if you're a worrier. Michelle Smith does not fit into that category. Neither does Erik de Bruin. They believed they had planned for every eventuality in Atlanta, including the early starts and the long days that are part and parcel of Olympic meets.

'The swim times were different from the norm in America,' explains Michelle. 'I am not a morning person. I don't swim very fast early in the day so I have to be awake a couple of hours before I'm ready to swim a heat. I'm an evening racer. In the morning heats you have to be alert enough not to make a mistake and miss the final. In Atlanta the heats started at 10 a.m. which is a little bit later than most of the other internationals, so we planned to be up at 7.30 a.m. or 8 a.m.'

'There is an inherent danger with a long day like the Olympics,' says Erik. 'You can get up really early and fade out by the end of the night for the final. There is a very thin line between energy and fatigue at that level of competition.'

Michelle continues: 'In most internationals, the finals start at 4 p.m. or 5 p.m.; but in Atlanta it was 7 p.m. If you were unlucky, your final could be on at 8.30 p.m. or 9 p.m. If you are up at 6 a.m. and have to swim a final at 8.30 p.m., it can be pretty hard going.'

That makes energy levels important. And diet all the more relevant.

Michelle says: 'Diet was one of the key areas Erik worked on when he took over my coaching. He was appalled at some of my habits. He revised my food intake and the benefits have been phenomenal. Now before races I don't eat too much apart from a lot of fish and rice with very little variation. I have breakfast, but not very much – maybe cornflakes and scrambled eggs.

'You have to be careful about what you eat for days before the competition. It is just as bad to get sick in the build-up as it is on the day of competition. You can't afford to start eating crazy things that you are not used to, just because you are in another country. I stuck to cornflakes and scrambled eggs – my staple diet.'

On that last night prior to competition, RTE television ran a preview to the Olympics back in Ireland. Michelle Smith was the support act; Sonia O'Sullivan the lead in the great drama ready to unfold. Most Irish fans favoured Sonia for at least one gold. Michelle was a contender; maybe a bronze medal would come her way if she was lucky. Four events seemed a tall order. Four medals seemed fantasy stuff, cuckoo land.

But not to Michelle Smith, and not to Erik de Bruin. They had a good feeling about the pool at the Georgia Tech. That night, before competition began, they had a good feeling about the Centennial Olympics, as Michelle recalls.

'I had good vibes about the pool and that was important. In our sport, there are fast pools and slow pools. This was a fast pool in my mind, after I had checked the turns, the walls and the wave-lines between the lanes. I was comfortable with the stadium, with the pool and with the turns. That too was reassuring.

'People often ask me about our turns. We know when to turn because most of the time you can see the wall. On the backstroke they have flags suspended over the pool five metres from the end. During practice, you count how many strokes it takes you once you pass the flag to get to the wall. In competition then, as soon as you pass the flags, you count one, two, three, and then you know it is time to turn. You also have to check the flags are five metres from the wall. That isn't always the case. That last practice night in Atlanta, I reckoned it was a fast pool; but it didn't really matter. It was going to be the same for everybody on the day. It only matters if you are going for a record. In the Olympics, we were going for medals.'

That's exactly what Michelle went for. And that night, before the first race of Atlanta '96, Michelle Smith fell asleep happy in the knowledge that her Olympic dream was about to become a reality. She went to bed with a positive mental attitude.

'I wasn't nervous,' Michelle says, 'I was quietly confident. In the weeks prior to the games, I made sure I was in good shape. I knew I could do a good 400-metre individual medley and possibly a worthy 200-metre butterfly, although, quite literally, I didn't know how good a 400-metre freestyle I was capable of until I went to Florida. I knew it was good, but not how good. At that moment I would have settled for one medal.'

Erik says: 'I was still thinking of the 400-metre freestyle; I knew Michelle could do a really good time there if she was entered for it. I was hoping for a medal in the 400-metre individual medley; I knew roughly what Michelle could swim, but I did not know about the others in contention. We had studied the field, but you never know what they are going to swim on the day. There are always one or two surprises, and one or two who surprise the other way and fail. You have a better idea after the heats when you can see who is fit.

'Of course you have the world rankings, and they give an indication of what people are capable of. It is only an indication, however, because Michelle, for example, wasn't rated for much of the year. The ratings are based on performances for the season. Three weeks before the Olympics she entered the ratings for the first time as number one in the 400-metre freestyle after her time at Pine Crest. She wasn't in the ratings at all for the 400-metre individual medley.'

Michelle adds: 'There is always an unknown factor at the games. With the Olympics, you will always have someone who will come out of nowhere, totally unexpected.'

Someone did just that at the Centennial Games. That someone was Michelle Smith.

Atlanta Diary

SATURDAY, 20 JULY

Expectation back home was high but not golden when it came to Michelle Smith and the heats for the 400-metre individual medley at the Georgia Tech Aquatic Centre, Atlanta. A nation passionate about sport, but with only a passing interest in swimming, looked to Sonia O'Sullivan to provide the main fix of gold medals at the Centennial Games.

This Smith girl was a bonus. If she did well in the first week of Olympic competition, the nation would rejoice. If she didn't? Well they'd all sit back and think of Sonia. Good old Sonia was a world champion in the big league. She ran for big money and big medals. She won most of them, the latter as well as the former. Michelle? Heck! Michelle was a swimmer, a different breed; a breed as dedicated and as fanatical as the cyclists who had done so much to light up Irish sport against the grain years earlier.

Roche and Kelly were looked on as being half-demented, yet half-inspired. They had to be a bit funny to put themselves through the torture of sitting on a saddle for hours on end when every self-respecting Irish kid was down at the local field doing what they were born to do – kicking a football with their friends against the enemy from the next parish.

Swimmers? Well, they were all the same, the same as the cyclists and the marathon runners. They lived in Irish sport's twilight zone. They got up ridiculously early in the morning to train. They swam up and down the same length of water in pools that only dreamt of 50-metre status. They got their parents and their coaches out of bed to pursue a sport that had never seen an Irish contestant qualify for

98

an Olympic final; a sport that had been bereft of silverware, goldware and even bronzeware until Gary O'Toole finished second in Bonn at the European Championships in 1989.

Swimming: a sport that had been denied an Irish champion until Michelle Smith went to Vienna in 1995 and twice struck gold at the European Championships; a sport that ranked in the Second Division of Irish interest until the summer of '95 when an Irish girl got into Viennese waters and swam her way to victory. That got Michelle Smith into the news headlines. It got swimming onto the front covers. It threatened to rock the status quo – which sorely needed rocking!

Significantly, Jack Charlton brought the Irish soccer team to the same Austrian sports site a month after Michelle's solid gold Sunday. He saw his team receive a European Championship roasting. The popularity of soccer that had been the sporting fix of the nation ten years previously was starting to decline. The poor relation called swimming was coming on the up.

Michelle Smith gave her nation reason to be cheerful when she was in the Austrian capital and was duly rewarded with the first real glimpse of recognition back home. The Irish soccer team lost just a short-course swim away from that pool and were rounded on by the critics as an era ground its weary way to a sad end. The sands were shifting in the direction of Rathcoole. Those sands were to move again on the morning of 20 July as Atlanta awoke to the first day of competition in the 1996 Olympic games.

Michelle Smith's first event was the 400-metre individual medley – four legs of 100 metres in four different disciplines: butterfly, backstroke, breaststroke and freestyle in that order. Michelle was already an accomplished force in the individual medley course. She had won the 'B' final over the distance at the World Championships in Rome in 1994. She had won silver in the discipline at the European Championships the following year. She was the fifth fastest of all the competitors entered in the event in Atlanta.

She was there, Ireland believed, to make the last eight and to make history, the first Irish swimmer ever to stand on the blocks in an Olympic final. Just as she had made history at the World Championships when she stood on the blocks in a final, the 200-metre butterfly, two years earlier. Just as she had made history with two golds in the Europeans the previous summer, victories over the

200-metre individual medley and the 200-metre butterfly. Her country merely expected Michelle Smith to break national records and to rewrite Irish sporting history again. But Michelle Smith believed she was there to win a gold medal.

Her pre-Olympic time helped in the draw for the heats of a distance that had been dominated for more years than they had all cared to remember by the great Hungarian Kriztina Egerszeggi, Michelle's conqueror in Vienna. Michelle Smith was drawn in heat number three alongside Metzler from America, Kurotori and Hiranaka from Japan, Chrastova from the Czech Republic, Yan from China, Vestergaard from Denmark and Rund from Germany.

Heats are the worry for every swimmer in a major finals. It is important to do enough to qualify; but it is equally important not to do too much so as to ruin your medal bid in the final. Too many great names have blown up in Olympic heats. Too many have been caught in slow heats, relaxed, and discovered that eight other swimmers in faster heats had faster times.

It could happen some day that eight swimmers from a really fast heat could post the best eight times and qualify for the final. There is always a risk factor involved with the heat system. It is staggered to keep the best swimmers and the best times apart. But only eight swimmers can contest any one final. And it has been known for big names and big strokes to miss out in the major championships. Michelle Smith was always aware of that in Atlanta.

She was also aware of the need for perfection. For four years, she had dedicated her life to her sport. She trained, she rested, she replaced foods and fluids, and then she trained some more. All this she did with only one aim in life: gold at the Atlanta Olympics.

On the morning of 20 July, Michelle Smith rose on time. She breakfasted according to plan – cornflakes and scrambled eggs in the Olympic canteen – all the food she needed to fuel that bid for glory. She jumped on a golf cart with her husband and her coach. Her heart began to beat to the rhythm of the race, the rhythm of the chase. Three-quarters of an hour before the heats of the 400-metre individual medley, the next Olympic champion jumped out of a golf cart and entered her theatre of dreams, bang on schedule.

As Michelle recalls, 'With all the Olympic hype, I didn't want to be hanging around for a long time in the stadium. Most of the time away from competition over there was spent outdoors, waiting in the heat and humidity, waiting for the call. With the morning sun at its highest at the time of the heats, there was a danger of over-exposure to the rays and to the humidity. We had to time it to perfection. I entered the pool complex as late as possible, just in time for the 20 or so minutes I needed in the warm-up pool, the five minutes or so to change into my lucky aquablade suit for the heat or the finals and the 15 minutes when you have to report officially for duty. Added together that schedule had me in the stadium 45 minutes before my race time – and that was plenty of time for me and for Erik.

'I felt really strong that first morning. I felt very concentrated and confident in the first heat. I wasn't overwhelmed; I knew what I had to do. The draw put me in the second last heat. I had to make sure I was fast enough to make the final but without expending too much energy. I had to be clever, to be harder and smarter than the rest. If I didn't need to put in 100 per cent, it would have been stupid to do so. At the same time, there is a fine line between knowing how much you can ease up and missing the final. I went pretty hard for the first 250–300 metres of the heat. In the last 100 metres I was far enough ahead to ease down and swim it far less frantically. I knew that if I didn't need the energy reserve that night then I would certainly need it at the end of the week.'

Michelle had no problems in her 400-metre individual medley heat. The Chinese girl, Yan Chen, had a faster personal best going to Atlanta; the American, Whitney Metzler, was the toast of the home crowd. Both played second fiddle to Michelle Smith in that heat.

She led from the gun, the prolific start that is such a feature of her style propelling her into the water ahead of the rest in the first 50 metres of the butterfly, taking the first turn well in front in a time of 29.50. At the end of the first 100 metres, she had increased that lead to one and a half lengths over Metzler, with Chen waiting her turn to pounce.

Metzler made ground over the breaststroke as Michelle's early dominance faltered slightly. It was to prove a false alarm. Michelle cruised in the final 100-metre freestyle. The training, the discipline, and the stamina imported into her swimming persona during the long days and long nights in Holland were paying off.

Metzler and Chen tried to catch Smith in those final 100 metres. Both failed. Smith cruised home, relaxing in the final metres as she kept an eye on Metzler, to win the heat in a time of 4:43.79. It was to be the third fastest time of the heats, beaten only by the reigning Olympic and European champion, Egerszeggi, and the girl the Hungarian had pipped in the final heat, Emma Johnson of Australia.

Michelle said, 'I felt pleased after the heat but not ecstatic. To win an Olympic medal you have to make the final so that was a relief in itself. It sounds silly; but if you're not in, you can't win. There are eight people in the final and as long as you're in there you've got a chance. I was also happy with my condition. I felt comfortable within myself, and I felt comfortable with the pool which was important. I knew I had frozen when I hit the starting blocks in Barcelona four years earlier. This time, there were no nerves, no anxieties. I stood on the blocks, shut out the stadium, the noise, and the hype of the Olympics. I swam my way into the final. There was a concern over my breaststroke leg when I allowed Metzler to gain ground, but I felt confident I could get that right in the final that night. The last 100 metres of the heat I took relatively easily. I knew I was ahead; I knew exactly what I needed to do to qualify. I knew the American girl was gaining ground, but I wasn't too worried about her.

'After the race, the journalists asked me about the Chinese girls who were getting criticised for their swims. I just said that I wasn't interested, that perhaps they were taking it easy. I said that I wanted to concentrate on my own race. With all the hype and the pressure, the Olympics is such an unpredictable event. I was only interested in seeing how I had done when I touched the wall at the end of the final that night.'

Michelle's winning time in that heat was 4:43.79, her fastest time of the year and almost a second and a half down on her personal best. But there was still room for improvement, and she knew it as she made her way back to the Irish block in the Olympic village after rewriting the history books that proud Georgian morning. She was the first Irish swimmer to make an Olympic final. That in itself was justification for self-contentment. There are those in Irish swimming who would have been content with that alone, but not Michelle Smith. She was a natural born winner. She was going to beat the best of them – Egerszeggi and all.

Michelle commented, 'I knew Kriztina Egerszeggi was going to be the one to beat. She had never been beaten before in a major championship. If I finished ahead of her it was quite likely I would win a medal. She simply doesn't swim in an event unless she thinks she is going to win it. The 200-metre backstroke is her dominant event, but in past championships, for example, she swam the 100-metre backstroke because she was sure she could win that.

'I knew if she was swimming the 400-metre individual medley, then she must have been thinking that she could win it. That's the type of fighter she is. She's only just 22, but she was an Olympic champion at 13, and has the mind and the will-power of a veteran. The American, Alison Wagner, the home crowd's own great hope for the race, was fast as well but I didn't know how tough she was.

'In an Olympic final, toughness, both mental and physical, can be everything. I knew Egerszeggi had the durability needed. Thanks to Erik's training programme I now had it as well. And I was ready to prove it to Egerszeggi, to Wagner, and to anyone else who fancied her chance.

'For the final, I was right beside Egerszeggi with the American, Wagner, on the other side of me. Egerszeggi had enjoyed lane advantage in Vienna when she was also beside me and was able to monitor my butterfly. She had watched me in the heats; so when it came to the European final, she ensured that she was up there with me for the butterfly, and then she did all the damage on the backstroke leg, her strongest. She knew my butterfly form. She knew what I had done in the Olympic heats, so I expected Egerszeggi to make a move in the butterfly, and then to try to pull away on the backstroke.

'Because her breaststroke isn't good she had to stay with me in the opening 100 metres of butterfly, get ahead of me in the backstroke, and then hope that she had done enough to hold me off for the final 200 metres. Tactically I knew exactly where I stood.'

In the past, Michelle Smith had turned to music to act as the back-drop to her pool ambition. In times of concentration, the Walkman piped Mary Black into her ears: in time of energetic fervour, it was the music of Tina Turner. In Atlanta, there was to be no music, just the constant thought of victory.

Michelle and Erik spoke about this power of thought: 'When Erik and I came to the pool for the final that evening we just carried on as if it was nothing special. We did our normal pre-race rituals, and we sat around the warm-up area cracking jokes and laughing. Psychologically speaking, the warm-up area and the call-room are very important. When you come into the swimmers' area at the stadium, the rest of the girls are looking at you, weighing you up, deciding if you are confident enough to win. If you look nervous, they will take advantage of that.'

'You have to play these mind games. Before the 400-metre individual medley, for example, I didn't help Egerszeggi much by walking right in front of her and looking deep into her eyes, to see if she had the hunger she was going to need to beat Michelle that night. You could almost call it eyeballing her!' said Erik.

'That was something Erik had used in his favour when he had competed in world-class athletics competition. He encouraged me to play mind games with the opposition. That was unheard of in swimming. Certainly nobody had ever tried to do it with me. They wouldn't have gotten close enough to succeed with Erik beside me. We always go somewhere where we can be by ourselves. Other swimmers wait in the warm-up pool with their coaches and then go into the call-room. We wait in the tunnel and find a place where we can be on our own without people walking past us.'

'I make sure that Michelle is the one with a really nice mat to lie down on to relax. The others all have to stand!' adds Erik.

This time, merely being able to compete was not going to be enough for Michelle Smith and her coach. This time, she was getting into an Olympic pool to win – and to win well! She would win for Michelle Smith; for Erik de Bruin; for her family; for her country.

Erik and Michelle discussed this. He said, 'When you go in there in the morning your job is to make the final – that is the only place where you can win medals. It's not like you go in there saying I am going to be happy whether or not I get to the final.'

Michelle continued: 'You look at it in two stages. The first stage is to make the final; then you forget about that and try to concentrate on winning a medal.'

'So it wasn't like you went in there just to make it to the final and then you got gold,' says Erik. 'But I think the reason you do that is you can make mistakes if you are already thinking about the final before you've made it.'

'Like Fransisca Van Almszick, the best swimmer in Germany. A couple of times in big championships, she has come in ninth after the heats and failed to make the finals; then she swims a world record in the "B" final.'

'She has done that a number of times; it is a psychological thing with her. I was determined it would not happen to me in the final,' concludes Michelle.

But no matter how strong the preparation, the Hungarian Egerszeggi was the big threat in that first race, the opponent who demanded respect with her awesome record over the distance stretching back to her first Olympic gold medal at the tender age of 13. There were also others in Michelle's company that Saturday night who were there to dive in and be counted, principally the great American hope, Alison Wagner, who had finished second when Michelle was ninth over the distance at the 1994 world finals in Rome.

The crowd of 15,000 were, in the majority, there to see Wagner lift the 400-metre individual medley crown. The neutrals had a feeling for the favourite, the champion Egerszeggi. The Irish, amongst them Michelle's parents, Brian and Pat, and her manager, Kathy Stapleton, made their voices heard above the din of American partisanship. In Rathcoole, Michelle's sisters Sarah and Aisling and brother Brian, when they weren't on RTE television, were the star attractions at the family local, The Poitin Still – the unofficial Irish swimming fans' headquarters for the duration of the Olympic games.

In Atlanta, the home crowd were left disappointed as events unravelled before their disbelieving eyes. Irish eyes were left as wet as the Georgian waters. Michelle Smith started her first Olympic final like a bullet. She was in first, her leap from the blocks propelling her ahead of the field before a breath was drawn. She led for the first 100-metre butterfly, traditionally one of her strongest allies in the individual medley class. Egerszeggi, conscious of Michelle Smith's strength and potential after their Vienna meeting the previous summer, knew her time would come on the backstroke, the stroke she had dominated for over a decade.

So it was in Atlanta as Egerszeggi and Wagner made their moves. The Hungarian made up ground on the second 50 metres of the back-stroke, and Wagner joined her assault on Michelle Smith's ambition in the third 100 metres, the breaststroke, the stroke that had been Michelle's weakest in the heat that morning. Others worried but not Michelle and not Erik, hunched down in the tunnel area below the pool as he watched his wife make her move for gold in the final 100 metres, the freestyle leg that was to launch her bid for glory.

Egerszeggi and Wagner were in front, but the stretch ahead of

Michelle was not impregnable. The hours in Dutch pools; the hours in Dutch gyms; the pains of defeats past; the Olympic dream – they all served to inspire Michelle Smith as she made the penultimate tumble-turn of her first Olympic final in Atlanta. The gold medal was calling a new daughter home.

As America and Hungary awaited a gold medal, Ireland snuck its nose in front. Michelle Smith stormed back into the lead on the changeover to freestyle, her front crawl eating at Egerszeggi's advantage and spitting it into the golden water. By the final turn, a tumble-turn perfected with the frog leaps that had caused so much merriment in a Dutch gymnasium, Michelle Smith was in front and in control. Egerszeggi looked for something else and found only the comforts of a bronze medal. Wagner attempted to give chase but abandoned hope and glory with 20 metres to go. Ireland's first swimming medal was guaranteed. Ireland's first swimming medal was gold. Ireland's first female gold medal was secured.

Michelle recalls, 'When we got into the pace of the first 100 metres, Egerszeggi was behind me – quite a bit behind me. I don't know if it was one or two seconds on the first 100 metres but I was surprised. My first split was a bit faster than normal, but it was still quite slow which made it surprising that Egerszeggi wasn't up there with me.' But, according to Erik, 'Prior to Atlanta, her butterfly had been poor enough. She did a 100-metre butterfly in Hungary before the Olympics and that was slow.'

Michelle continues: 'That time from her was 1:02.7 which was comforting for me going into the final. If that was the best time she could do in a sprint this year, then she wasn't going to be able to do that in the opening 100 metres of a 400-metre medley. If she had done a sprint like that in the opening 100 metres, she wouldn't have finished the race.

'That gave me confidence going to the blocks. But we had also decided on a very careful plan for the final. I was to be aware of Egerszeggi. I was not to be afraid of her. That was crucial. To win the race I had to concentrate on my own swim. If I did that, and it was good enough, I would be an Olympic champion.

'Having seen that she was behind after that first leg, I had to forget about her and concentrate on my own race. She caught up with me on the backstroke as I knew she would, but she didn't gain anything like the ground I feared and, I'm sure, that she had expected.

'I was up there with her going into the breaststroke. Then, I knew I could win the gold medal. As long as I was within a second of her at that stage, I knew my fitness would see me through. I had done the work in the gym. I had put up the hours in the pool. I had made sacrifices for this moment. As long as Kriztina Egerszeggi was within my sight at the turn for the freestyle, I could catch her and beat her. I knew that going to the turn.

'I could see them when I was breathing – I could see Egerszeggi and Wagner. They were up there and I was right up there with them. Going into the last 100 metres there were three of us together. For a split second, I thought I might win. After that split second, I forgot about winning and went back to concentrating on my race plan. I couldn't lose concentration in the last 100 metres. When I had tumble-turned for the final 50 metres of the freestyle and had seen myself moving forward, then I knew they weren't going to catch me.

'But I still had to keep putting my head down to go for the last 50 metres. Some commentators reckoned I slowed down and that's rubbish! I don't know anybody who slows down in an Olympic final when they are racing for a medal.

'It is almost impossible to describe the feeling hitting the wall with nobody beside me. At first I was totally ecstatic. I thought I had done enough to win. I turned around and saw number one behind my name. A couple of seconds later, the realisation hit me: I was an Olympic champion!

'Then I was in a little bit of shock. There was almost a sense of disbelief there. This was something I had aspired to for so many years; something I had put so much work into; something I had dreamed of; something Erik had dreamed of; something my family had dreamed of. When you have actually achieved your goal it leaves a feeling of shock.

'The immediate aftermath is still a daze. I don't think Egerszeggi was very happy but she did congratulate me. She finished third in the end. Wagner was second. She wasn't happy either, I think she thought she was going to win it.'

Michelle Smith's time of 4:39.18 was the fastest in the world in 1996 and a new Irish record. Her split time for the final 100 metres, the freestyle leg, was the fastest in a 400-metre individual medley in the history of swimming.

But all those statistics are irrelevant. Even now they mean little.

Michelle Smith was an Olympic champion – at last. It was a job well done, both for swimmer and for coach.

Erik recalls, 'I watched the final race downstairs on TV as the stands were full. I didn't even think about a seat in the stands until Michelle went into the call-room and I thought, "Where do I go now?" First, I went down to the TV area, and they told me to go upstairs and see if there were any seats left; but every seat was full. They won't let you stand at the side of the pool; you cannot get in if there is not a seat for you. I had to watch on a television with a load of other people downstairs – below the pool area – and it was nerve wracking.

'I desperately wanted Michelle to win. I knew she could win. I believed she would win. But there was nothing I could do about it.

'If you are an athlete, you are in control. When you are a coach, you have done your work; and now your athlete has to do it. That's very hard because you are standing there helpless. You cannot do anything. I wasn't screaming at the television; I was just crying . . . crying, crying as she raced to the line in front.

'I am not ashamed of that. At the breaststroke stage, I knew she had it won, I knew that in the last 100 metres she would pull clear and win by at least two or three metres on the other swimmers.

'I was surrounded by other coaches and swimmers, and people from the organising committee. At first they didn't know what was happening to me; and then I said, "That's my wife swimming there!" And then they started applauding and congratulating me. Then I wanted to see Michelle, but that was a bit of a problem because they don't just let you walk onto the pool deck. There were about four or five security people trying to stop me; but I think I took them by surprise! I ran onto the pool deck and waved to Michelle, then I ran back and apologised to them. We didn't get to embrace until afterwards.'

Here Michelle took up the story. 'It takes a couple of minutes again before you can meet your coach with all the television requirements at the poolside. At first it was the BBC, then French TV, and then a few others before I even got near Erik.

'It was emotional hugging him after winning the gold medal. He had cried during the race; but I didn't after that victory, even when he threw his arms around me and we realised what had just happened. I didn't cry until after the very last race – when it was all over. Then I got very emotional. I found the combination of excitement and nerves made me really, really happy. I was ecstatic and threw my arms around Erik; I don't think I let go of him for about two minutes!'

Erik laughed: 'Until I was going blue in the face!'

Then Michelle continued: 'There were no tears then. I saw my manager immediately afterwards because she had managed to bribe most of the security guards in the swimming arena to get herself right beside the pool deck. Normally you have to stay sitting in your seat, but she was running up and down after every race, waving her arms. It's only afterwards that you take time to look around the crowd and pick people out. There were coaches there from different countries that I knew. They waved and congratulated me.

'I saw my parents in the stands but didn't get to meet them until the Olympic Council reception that night. They were bawling their eyes out. I still wasn't crying as I was really enjoying it, it was one of the happiest moments in my life, and I did just that, I enjoyed it. I took the time to look around, to wave at people who were carrying tricolours, to wave at people I knew, the coaches I had trained with in Canada and America, and to wave at my family and friends up in the crowd.'

In the immediate aftermath of the gold medal swim Michelle Smith became the centre of media attention at the Georgia Tech pool. 'I did a couple of interviews by the side of the pool immediately after the race,' she said, 'and then I had to rush past the waiting newspapermen and into the swim-down pool. I had to get that swim down done before the press conference or I would not have been able to swim in the remaining three races. I'm sure that was hard for some of the press people to understand because they naturally wanted me to stand and talk straightaway. I could have stayed there for an hour. As it was, I had only 25 minutes before the presentation, 25 minutes to enjoy it, to savour the atmosphere, to lap it all up.

'It is hard to describe my feelings at the presentation. I was thrilled that I had achieved a dream. I can never go higher than winning an Olympic gold medal. No matter what happens, nobody can ever take it away from me. That had been my dream come true.

'It was also thrilling to see the tricolour go up and hear them play "Amhran na bhFiann". I know there was controversy at home over the speed they played the anthem, but I couldn't care less what version they used. I was so wrapped up in the emotion of it all that it didn't dawn on me that the speed was wrong, nor did I realise the magnitude of the occasion, of the fact that I was the first Irish woman to win a medal. The crowd that first night certainly appreciated it.

'The press conference came straight after the medal ceremony. The first one was pretty easy as most of the reporters were in shock. Nobody had expected me to win it. They had expected Egerszeggi to win, so the press didn't know what to ask me. Except, that is, Sean Ban Breathnach from Radio na Gaeltachta who shocked the Americans when he asked me a question in Irish. I cannot remember exactly what he asked, but then again I cannot remember a lot of the questions at that conference.

'Erik was anxious for me to get away from the press conference as soon as possible. It was a great thrill to sit there as an Olympic champion, but he was very conscious of the fact that I had another race two days later.'

Celebrations in the Smith camp were minuscule. The proudest husband and wife in Atlanta managed just one glass of mineral water at a party thrown in their honour by the Olympic Council of Ireland. Their appearance was brief.

Michelle explains, 'The Olympic Council of Ireland held a reception to mark the win. I was conscious that it was the first day, Ireland's first medal and it was a gold. Pat Hickey had asked us to drop in, even for a few minutes, and we didn't want to let anybody down. We agreed to attend on the provision that I could get away quickly. I was bleary eyed after the events of the day. All I wanted was some food and some sleep.

'The other bonus of the reception was the chance to see my parents for the first time after the race. If anything, they were even more emotional about the whole thing than I was. Just to see them and to share the moment with them was something to treasure.

'After a few quick minutes with them, we went back to the Olympic village, grabbed something to eat, and went back to the Irish block. But the adrenalin was still flowing. It was difficult to come down. We didn't sleep too well that night. It was very hard to come down from the high of an Olympic gold medal. It was all worth it.'

Atlanta Diary

SUNDAY, 21 JULY

An air of disbelief blew in with the winds coming off the Atlantic and the Irish Sea that Sunday morning. Ireland awoke with the memories of an Olympic gold medal in its midst. At least that's what people thought they had remembered from the night before. For that split second before memory became a reality, thousands awoke with a recollection of a gold medal for Michelle Smith in the Olympic pool, Atlanta. And as soon as they switched on their radios, turned on their television sets or opened their eyes and minds to their favourite Sunday sports papers or newspapers, they knew they were right. Their eyes hadn't deceived them. Ireland had won a gold medal on the first day of competition at the Atlanta games. The recipient had been Michelle Smith of Rathcoole, Co. Dublin.

By the end of the day, they knew all that there was to know about Michelle Smith; her husband, the man the media dubbed 'stern-faced Erik'; her father, Brian, and mother, Pat; her sisters, Sarah and Aisling; her brother, Brian. They had all become media stars in their own right.

From Clonakilty in County Cork to Gweedore in Donegal, a nation celebrated. From Atlanta to the Amazon, the world acclaimed the story of 'the little woman from Rathcoole' as Michelle was later to dub herself.

People who'd never known the difference between the deep and shallow ends were talking about 50-metre pools, Lotto funding for sport, and the training facilities in Holland as if their lives depended on it.

RTE television re-ran George Hamilton's interview with Michelle and Erik. It seemed as if they re-ran the finish to that race the night before a thousand times. Each time she won. She told the nation that she was proud. She told the nation that watching the tricolour going up at the medal ceremony was the best feeling in the world.

The nation reciprocated.

President Mary Robinson said: 'Michelle Smith is a superb role model for all young sports people. Her gold medal is an historic achievement.'

Taoiseach and Fine Gael leader John Bruton said: 'The gold is just reward for all Michelle's effort and endeavour over the last four years. I congratulate her.'

Tanaiste and Labour Party leader Dick Spring broke a journey to Indonesia on EU business to say: 'I share the country's joy. I hope this magnificent start to the games will inspire our other competitors.'

The Minister for Sport, Bernard Allen, was in Atlanta to witness Michelle's gold medal success. At the Irish party to celebrate her achievement he said: 'Michelle has shown the world what a great athlete she is. We have known and admired her dedication for years now. Her gold medal is a milestone in Irish sporting achievement.'

The Olympic Council of Ireland president, Pat Hickey, had admired the gold medal as Michelle paid a quick visit to the victory celebrations the night before. 'It is a phenomenal achievement. You don't see too many of those medals walking around Ireland,' said Hickey.

Back in Dublin the owner of a landmark public house on the N7, the main road from Dublin to the South, was clearing up from the night before. The Poitin Still had long been the Smith family's local in Rathcoole. The pub is proud of its links with Michelle Smith and her family, so proud that the landlord, Louis Fitzgerald, paid for Brian and Pat Smith to fly out to America, to be poolside when their daughter went for the gold. He was repaid a million times over when Michelle captured that first medal for Irish swimming, for Irish women.

The cameras were out in force at The Poitin Still. Michelle's sisters, Sarah, 24, and Aisling, then 18, and younger brother, Brian, nine, watched the gold medal race in the comfort of the lounge, surrounded by a galaxy of aunts, uncles, cousins and friends, both new and old. 'We didn't get to bed until 5.30 a.m. All the training and the effort has paid off for Michelle. We are all delighted for her,' said Sarah on radio that Sunday. 'I'm not surprised. Michelle's always done anything she has put her mind to.'

Aisling revealed the confidence of the family circle as they had sat in front of their various television screens the night before. 'After watching her win her heat, I was sure she was going to get a medal. Now I believe she can win medals in the three events to come. I'd lay money on it. She's on a high now. She's a battler and will go for it in every race.'

Young Brian was still bleary-eyed when the microphones caught up with him. 'I am exhausted, but it was worth it,' he said. 'When I woke up this morning, I wasn't sure if I was dreaming. Michelle was incredible.'

Over in Atlanta, dad Brian was still coming to terms with his new-found status in life as the father of an Olympic champion. 'I never doubted she'd get the gold medal. I have dreamed of this race all year, always with this result. The whole family is so proud of her.'

For all the euphoria outside the Olympic village, in Atlanta and in Ireland, there was an element of realism in one pocket of Olympic City. Michelle Smith and Erik de Bruin were also up early that Sunday; not to celebrate but to prepare. The hard work was only beginning.

Michelle said, quite matter of fact: 'The next morning we were back in the pool. That's the schedule we always adhere to in competition. The fact that I had won an Olympic gold medal the night before was irrelevant. There were three more gold medals there to be won. My schedule was more important than the euphoria surrounding that first medal. The schedule was all important. So was our privacy.

'That morning, Erik had said that he wanted me to swim continuously for half an hour just to get the lactic acids out of my muscles. Immediately afterwards, I got a massage from Marie Elaine Grant, who normally works in the Blackrock Clinic. She was with the Irish team in Atlanta and she was very good. She looked after me for the whole week, and gave me a massage twice a day, something which I really needed with such a busy schedule.'

Erik chipped in. 'That was one of the things that was badly organised at the European Championships in Vienna. There was no physio for Michelle so we had to ask the delegates from other countries if we could borrow theirs. Some of them would say "no", but the physio would say "okay", so we had to go somewhere where nobody could see us for Michelle to get a rubdown after the races. That part of things was really badly organised by the IASA in Vienna.

'For Atlanta, we requested a masseur twice a day. Winning gold medals is not supposed to be sore, just nice. Michelle needed that.'

Michelle continued, 'After that first swim on Sunday, we had lunch in the Olympic cafeteria and then I had a little sleep for two hours or so. I always do that in the afternoon as part of my normal routine; so I tried to keep the same routine in Atlanta. I also felt that I needed the rest badly. The previous night had been late, so I needed extra sleep. I went to the Dutch block because I could be on my own there. There were too many people looking for me in the Irish section of the village.'

Michelle and Erik brought an extra piece of luggage with them to his sister's quarters that Sunday afternoon. It was an Olympic medal, a gold Olympic medal.

Michelle explains, 'We gave the medal to Erik's sister, Corrie, for safe-keeping and she put it in a drawer in her room. We figured that people would know I had a medal. If they knew where the Irish block was, they could find out where my room was. If they wanted to break in and steal the gold medal, they could work out very easily where it was likely to be. We figured nobody would think that Erik's sister had my medal shoved in her drawer.' But: 'It was only later that we found out that the cleaners of the Dutch block had stolen hundreds of dollars and credit cards from between the clothes in the drawers. So it wasn't that safe after all!' Erik concluded.

Between rests, Michelle and Erik worked hard on the preparations for her next event, the 400-metre freestyle. At that stage, she was entered for the race as far as they were concerned. They weren't interested in the controversy over the timing of her entry. That was someone else's concern.

All they wanted to do was to prepare for another race, to wipe away the memory of that superb Saturday, and to prepare Michelle Smith for a magic Monday. Again, it was mind over body. She had trained for four years for this. She had dedicated a life to swimming for this. She had turned in the fastest time in the world that year for this event. Gold beckoned – but only if her attitude was right.

Michelle said: 'Sunday was "rest day"; but that was only a convenient term as far as we were concerned. Next day was the 400-

metre freestyle. I had to make a big effort to forget about the first race. I couldn't get too involved or excited about winning the medal. I had to wipe out any inquisitiveness about events back home. I had to be mentally right for another big challenge, for another Olympic final. That night, in my own mind, I went to bed with no memory of an Olympic gold. I was starting all over again the next morning.'

Ireland's Olympic account had opened with a gold medal, the first of any colour for an Irish woman, the first ever in the pool. To think that Michelle Smith could follow that with gold in the 400-metre freestyle was just too good to be true. Or was it?

Atlanta Diary

MONDAY, 22 JULY

Michelle Smith slept soundly in the heart of the Irish camp as Olympic history was rewritten on the night of Sunday, 21 July, and into the early hours of Monday. For the first time ever an Olympic arbitration committee sat to decide the fate of a swimmer, entered for the 400-metre freestyle heats to be held the next morning. That swimmer's name was Michelle Smith.

The United States, Germany and Holland had officially protested her acceptance for the race after a weekend of argument and counter argument. At 9.30 p.m. on Sunday, the Irish delegation received an order to attend the tribunal. They knew the Americans had serious reservations over Smith's acceptance for the event. The emergence of the Dutch and the Germans as dissenting voices was news to them.

The Olympic Council chief, Pat Hickey, and his secretary, Dermot Sherlock, flew the flag for Ireland at the meeting. Michelle slept on; her manager, Kathy Stapleton, waiting anxiously in room 207 of the Comfort Suite Inn two miles away for news of her entry. Hickey had fought Smith's corner on the issue for two days now. He had appealed to the IOC president, Juan Samaranch, to let her swim. That night in Atlanta, the heroic Hickey swung the decision. Sensing the German and Dutch swimming associations were acting without the authority of their Olympic Councils, he asked them that very question. They stuttered answers – and the jury came down in Ireland's favour. At 3 a.m., Ireland's gold medal hero was cleared to compete in the heats of the 400-metre freestyle seven hours later.

Michelle Smith slept on.

'I was oblivious to the whole thing. Just as I had to wipe out the memory of the gold medal on the Saturday, so I had to forget about the entry problem and get on with preparing for a new race at the Olympic games, a race which I had spent four years preparing for. I had to prepare for it as if I was going to swim the 400-metre freestyle. If that became a reality, then great! If it didn't, I would switch my attention to the next two races I was definitely entered for. I had to dismiss all thought of that fastest time in the world for the distance at Pine Crest a fortnight earlier. I had to forget that I had swum a 4:08 when there was a possiblity of not competing and of someone else winning it in a slower time with me watching enviously from the stands.

'None of that mattered. When I went to bed on the Sunday night, I knew I was competing the next day. I didn't know of an appeal and I didn't care. I was focused only on the chance of another medal.'

'That's exactly what I told Michelle,' says Erik, 'that she might as well forget about it and see what came out of it. If she had spent time getting worked up about the subject, it would have just wasted energy. The village was full of rumour. We were in, we were out; there were appeals, there were protests. The only thing we didn't hear about was the arbitration. That was probably just as well.'

'We might have lost sleep knowing it was going on until 2 a.m. or 3 a.m.,' says Michelle. 'It was only on the morning of the race that I was told about the arbitration, and that I was in. It was good news because, mentally, I had already been preparing for the race.

'I had one gold medal in my possession already and the chance of another medal at least. Whatever happened, I couldn't go wrong once they let me compete.'

Erik's view is that, 'You should always try to see something positive in everything. That first gold medal gave Michelle confidence. The decision to let her race was another event in her favour. If she had lost the first race I would have told her to use it as a spur, to gain revenge. Instead she went into those heats in good shape mentally and physically. Before the heats, I had told her to go and do it all over again.'

She did. In the morning heats, Smith swam a comfortable 4:09 but was beaten at the post by another German, Kristin Kielgass. More importantly the fastest heat of the day took its toll on two of Smith's big rivals with Dagmar Hase and Holland's Carla Guerts both involved.

Michelle explains: 'This was always going to be a big race, and not just because there were two Olympic champions in the field for the heats: the 1988 champion Janet Evans of America and the 1992 champion, Dagmar Hase from Germany. That meant the Olympic champions from the last two games were in this event and that was guaranteed to make it tough. I avoided them in the heats – thanks to my time in Florida – but I knew this was the one race where heat times could prove vital. We had to keep a check on the other three heats so that I knew exactly what I needed to do to make the final.'

'They were also different competitors,' adds Erik. 'There were two girls in there who could do a really fast last 50 or 100 metres so if they felt that they had a good chance, they would put up a very good fight.'

'I was in the very last heat,' continues Michelle, 'and Erik worked out that I needed a time of about 4:10 to be sure of qualifying; that was almost as good as my best ever time in Florida a fortnight earlier, the best time in the world this year. I also knew that I needed to hold something back for the final. It was a two-edged sword.'

Michelle Smith didn't wear her gold medal into the call-room before the final of the 400-metre freestyle. But she might as well have.

Michelle continues: 'The other competitors were afraid after the result of the 400-metre individual medley. Erik reckoned they were pysched out by the result of that race, and I had to use it to my advantage when we went into the call-room. It gave me confidence, the arrogance to strut around the call-room in the final seconds before the race. Erik had trained me to look cool and relaxed when I got out of the pool after the heats, even if I was exhausted. That also gave the competition something to think about. The right mental attitude is so important in those situations. And as Erik had proven when he walked up to Egerszeggi and had had a good long look at her, before the 400-metre individual medley, it helped to play a mind game or two as well. Not that the opposition had any chance of doing it with me – he wouldn't let them near me before the races.'

The heat produced the desired result for Michelle but not the performance her coach wanted. She had ended up in a race with the German Kristin Kielgass. Erik wondered how much it had taken out of her.

'The heat went well but I was a bit worried afterwards about that time of 4:09,' says Michelle. 'Kielgass had finished only marginally slower than Hase in the German trials. In the heat, she was in the lane next to me and swam her fastest, even coming up to the last 100 metres when I had tried to ease off a little bit. She got into a race with me in the last 100 metres and I didn't want to do that. I just wanted to do enough to qualify. So she beat me by one one-hundredth of a second. Erik asked me in the warm-up pool afterwards just how much the time had taken out of me. I was confident the effect was only minimal, but it was too early to tell at that stage.

'Prior to the 4:08, my best time had been 4:26; that was to come back to haunt me once Janet Evans had been eliminated. The reason for that time is that I never took the 400-metre freestyle seriously as an event, and the only time I had swum it was in April 1995. After I had swum the World Cup series, I took a month off. In April, the club in Holland asked me to swim the 400-metre freestyle because they were doing a league and needed the points. At that stage, I had been eight weeks out of the water and wasn't fit. I did the race in 4:26; you don't have to be a once in a lifetime writer about swimmers to know that that was not a good time, never mind a great time. It was, though, a time that came back to haunt me subsequently.'

'That time was used as ammunition against Michelle,' says Erik. 'It was unfair because last year, before the Europeans for example, she did the 100-metre freestyle at the Irish Nationals in a really fast time of 54 seconds – world-class standard. If you combine that with the 4:42 she did in the 400-metre individual medley, you can more or less calculate that Michelle could have swam the 400-metre freestyle last year at 4:11 or 4:12 at a tapered part of the season. Before Vienna, she was tapered, rested and ready to swim fast; so she would have done 4:11 or 4:12 had she entered the race at the European Championships. That looks a lot better than 4:26 but it is not fair to compare the two. If you look at the 400-metre individual medley in Vienna, the time there was 4:42, and in Atlanta it was 4:39; that's only three seconds' difference.'

Michelle says that she wasn't that concerned about the heat time. 'I was happy that I had kept enough in reserve for the final. Even though I had not given it 100 per cent, I still knew I would feel it in the last 100 metres of the 400-metre freestyle final. As an event, it is easier than the individual medley, where you start with the butterfly and move both arms together; the stroke rhythm is slower. Then you change to the backstroke where both arms are going at different speeds so that the rhythm is faster. Breaststroke is slower again, and then the freestyle is faster. In the medley, you are changing rhythms all the time, which is very hard to do. But with the freestyle, it is all the one rhythm, you just keep going and going and going.'

The rhythm of the Olympics was to change for Michelle Smith that morning. Back home in Ireland, the sports headlines were dominated by her achievement in qualifying for a second final. In America, just one piece of news merited attention – the fall from grace of one Janet Evans.

Michelle takes up the story: 'Because my heat was the last one, I knew I had made the final as I went over to do a poolside interview with Sharon Davies, who was working in Atlanta for the BBC. It was Sharon who told me that Janet Evans had been knocked out. I knew that would be a big blow to the Americans. She finished ninth; if you do that, you're out. She said she had miscalculated the time; but I don't think she could have swum much faster. I think she had swum only a second faster in the American trials but, judging by her 800 metres later on in the week, she wasn't in any shape to swim faster.'

'Janet Evans was in tears in the warm-up pool after the heat, she was hurting badly,' recalls Erik.

Michelle says: 'As soon as I got out of the water they flashed up the finalists to the crowd and flashed her up as ninth. That's when the bitching started. All of a sudden she was out of the final after all the media hype about how she was going to win her fifth Olympic gold to add to the three she had won in Seoul and the one in Barcelona.'

Evans and America needed a scapegoat. Her name was Michelle Smith.

Erik says that, 'They picked on Michelle because of the so-called late entry. They figured that if she had not swum then Evans would have been eighth.'

'She would not have won a medal though from the outside lane judging by the way she had swum all week,' adds Michelle.

While Michelle Smith prepared for more Olympic glory that night, Janet Evans took the gold medal for bitchiness – in a field of one. It did not deter the girl from Rathcoole, who was oblivious to the row developing in the outside world as she concentrated on a new golden dream. It worked.

Michelle had expected her main threat in the final to come from Germany's Dagmar Hase and Costa Rica's Claudia Poll. But Poll was feeling the after-effect of the previous day's 200-metre freestyle final when she had won by out-touching the German superstar, Franzisca Van Almsick. Instead it was the Dutch girl, Carla Guerts, who led the way until a sensational mid-race breakaway saw Michelle Smith taking the lead just after the 200-metre mark, and opening up a near unassailable lead at 300 metres before maintaining her form all the way to the line. Her winning time of 4:07.25 was the ninth fastest in history, and it smashed the Irish record she had set in Pine Crest only a fortnight earlier. Michelle Smith had won by a full second from Dagmar Hase of Germany, the winner of the gold medal over the same disance at the Barcelona Olympics. The bronze medal went to Kirsten Vlieghuis of Holland.

Michelle Smith had paced herself to perfection, allowing Carla Guerts of Holland to lead through the first 100 metres in a fast 60.1 seconds. Guerts was still in front at 200 metres in the time of 2:03.37, but Michelle was now on her shoulder, waiting to pounce. She now upped the tempo, and, by the next turn, Guerts was lagging behind and Smith had opened up a gap. By the 300-metre turn, the gold medal was guaranteed for Ireland as Smith enjoyed a two and a half second lead on the champion, Hase. Michelle Smith had done it again.

Michelle explains: 'For the final, we knew that there was not going to be much difference between all the swimmers in the first 200 metres; everybody was going to be pretty much on the level. The 1992 Olympic champion, Dagmar Hase, was very strong on the last 100 metres, and particularly the last 50 metres. She was a real champion and fighter; if she had had a smell of being within range of winning a medal or beating you, she would have really fought in the last 50 metres. I knew I could not let her be in that position in the last 50 metres. We had planned for me to keep my own pace for the first 200 metres, to stay with the pack, and then to make the break on the third 100 metres.'

'It was a completely different pace to that Michelle would normally swim,' adds Erik, 'but this was a race to win, and not a race for the fastest time. If you were to swim for a fast time, it would have been really stupid to change the pace. Instead, Michelle won the race on the 200–300-metre leg.'

'I built up a lead of a couple of metres after the 300-metre mark,' recalls Michelle. 'It was a good job I did as I had not gone as fast for the last 100 metres as the previous 100-metre leg. Thankfully, I still had enough of a lead by then and the others couldn't catch up with me. Hase did start to come back in the last 50 metres, but I had built up too big a lead; it was just too much for her. That was the plan. If I had been with her at 300 metres, I would have lost it – so it was a tactical race. The Dutch girl, Vlieghuis, got the bronze, and Kielgass, the German who had beaten me by one hundredth of a second in the heats and qualified with the fastest time, didn't make a medal at all.'

Erik continues: 'You can see from that result that Kielgass had given too much in the last 100 metres of the heat. So when she had needed it that night, it was gone. The time was 4:07.2: it was the fastest for the last four years, but it was a tactical race, not a speed one.'

Michell says that the achievement was as good as getting the first medal but the experience was different. 'When I had finished and touched the wall, I was still thrilled at the fact that I had won a second gold medal – but it will still never match the feeling of that first time you touch the wall and realise you are an Olympic champion. You can never match that again.

'From that moment on, the media spotlight really focused on me. They were behind the barriers screaming at me for interviews, shouting at me at the training pool. I was double Olympic champion. It felt good.'

Michelle's parents, Pat and Brian, were at the poolside again that night. They too became a focal point for media attention. Pat told the press: 'We were jumping up and down, on the edge of our seats. It was absolutely terrific! She's just brilliant!' Brian added: 'We are absolutely thrilled because tonight, when she had won her double, we realised that she is probably the greatest Irish female athlete ever. We wouldn't have missed this for anything. We are on top of the world!' The Olympic Council of Ireland chief, Pat Hickey, joined in the praise. He told NBC: 'Michelle proved tonight that she is an Olympic great. She told me before the race that she was going to excel in the pool – and she did.'

Michelle's immediate reward for winning her second gold medal of the Olympic Games was condemnation. She was condemned by Janet Evans and rounded on by the American media. She had beaten the rest of the field for that final. More importantly, in relation to the events as they unfolded, she had helped to explode the Janet Evans myth. The price of that explosion was heavy as Michelle describes.

'I was singled out as the wicked witch when Janet Evans failed to qualify for the final. She went straight to the American media and called a press conference which is not the norm for an athlete beaten at that stage of competition. After the heats, I had lunch, went for a sleep and did my usual post-heat and pre-race things before the final. I was neither aware of the press conference nor of anything she had said. It was only at my own press conference, after swimming the final and winning the medal, when people started asking me what I thought of Janet Evans's remarks, that I knew about her press conference. I had to say that I had no idea what they were talking about. They related quotes from her saying that she didn't know whether somebody who was 26 years of age could improve so much. She didn't think it was possible, saying, "People get worse with age but I guess some people get better." She was going round in circles saying, "There are a lot of accusations going on around the poolside, and I'm not making any of them, but . . ."

'I think the American press jumped on it because all of a sudden they had a story and it was easy copy. They tried to provoke me into getting into some sort of a cat-fight which I was never going to do. The only thing I did was to defend myself because I wasn't going to sit there and listen to all this being said about me.

'I was prepared for it. I knew after my 400-metre freestyle swim in Florida that I was a threat to Janet Evans. There had been so much hype about her – a lot of which she had generated herself – so I knew that once I had done the 400 metres in Pine Crest, I was going to come in for criticism in the States. I was ready for the hammering when I walked into that press conference. But I was more or less left to my own devices when they started throwing questions at me. My attitude was simple. I could either refuse to answer their questions and go off in a huff or I could sit there and listen to them and answer all of them in the most rational way I could. That's exactly what I did. I felt I could justify my case if I sat there and explained to them how I had trained, rested, ate, lived my life – these were all reasonable and rational explanations as to why I had improved.

'The Americans were also trying to make out that I had come out of nowhere. If I had sat there and said nothing I would have been guilty by insinuation. So I explained that I have been improving for the last three and a half years. I took them through my career details for 1995. That year, I had gone to number one in the world rankings at the end of the short-course season when I won the World Cup series. At the end of the '95 season I was number two in two events of the long course – the 200-metre individual medley and the 400-metre individual medley – after the European Championships. So how could they make out that I had come from nowhere?

'I did try to explain, but it was probably all a waste of time. The American press asked me the questions but didn't use my answers. They just wrote their own articles, regardless of what I had said. Thankfully there was a clear difference between the American media and the rest of the world's. The Irish looked after me as I had expected them to. The Australians and British were really good to me. The Europeans listened to what I had to say and took it all in.

'The Americans were on another planet. One reporter asked me a question, then turned around and started talking to her colleague while I was answering her question. The Stateside public didn't like the way their media treated me either. Most of the Americans I met in Atlanta, Boston and New York afterwards apologised for the way I had been handled by the American media; they said that they were genuinely sorry about the gutter press, that they really appreciated what I had done.

'I can't deny that the accusations – and the way they were put – hurt. I think it hurt me more afterwards than during the games when the hype of the races to come and the achievement of those gold medals kept me buzzing. But it still hurts.

'The fact that Janet Evans subsequently flopped in the 800 metres vindicated my theory that she was a spent force trying to blame anyone she could find for the passing of her time. She hasn't put me off America for life but she sure tried. I will race there again if I'm invited. And if Janet Evans wants to come out of retirement and take me on she can feel more than free to do so.

'The American press did everything they could to justify Evans's "sore loser" point of view. They went around the Olympic village and pool looking for anyone who had ever worked with me, spoken to me, or seen me. They wanted dirt, and they were prepared to go to any lengths to look for it. The vindication for me – and the satisfaction – was the fact that they couldn't find any.

'They tracked down my Canadian coach, Pierre Lafontain, in the stands. They traced another Canadian guru, Deryk Snelling, in the crowd. They found swimmers who had worked with me in Canada and America. They asked them all the same questions about my ability, about my improvements. They got the same answers. I sat back smugly as, one after another, they said that I was the toughest competitor they had ever met, the hardest trainer, the most determined athlete in their experience. That felt good.'

Naturally, the world press raked through the coals of Michelle's past. And they zoomed in on the case history of her husband and coach.

'Erik did not come into the press conferences but I knew well in advance that somebody was going to ask about him and his ban,' says Michelle. 'When it happened I just said that I was happy to answer any questions about me and my swimming but nothing else.'

Erik de Bruin stayed in the background in the midst of the Evans furore. His only purpose in life for that week in Atlanta was to coach his swimmer to Olympic gold. He was not there to deflect innuendo, to answer questions or to ask them. He was there to protect his swimmer and her gold medal ambition.

Erik says that, 'I hadn't seen any of Janet Evans's press conference either; I was still waiting for Michelle at the warm-up pool, waiting to get back to the rooms. I wasn't interested in what she had to say. I had no inclination either to listen to the nonsense coming from Evans. I am only interested in winning medals in the pool. You don't get medals for what goes on outside the pool. Janet Evans should know that.

'I had told Michelle that if she did well they would try to break her because she was a threat to them. I had told her that they would try to insult her and get at her mentally. It helped her that she was prepared for it when the onslaught came.'

Prepared or not, it was the ferocity of the attack that shocked Michelle Smith and Erik de Bruin. They had never experienced anything like it.

'No, I had never had anything thrown at me like those insinuations before. When I won two gold medals and a silver last year at the European Championships, I never got one such comment from another competitor. Or from the press. It hurt to be treated like that – by the Americans and by some of my own people. It will always hurt.'

Atlanta Diary

TUESDAY, 23 JULY

The morning after the night before. Michelle Smith awoke to find the world looking in and looking on as a great American heroine pointed the finger in only one direction. Janet Evans blamed everyone but herself for her Olympic failure. Sadly, she chose to blame Michelle Smith more than anyone else. She ignored the fact that seven other swimmers had also finished in faster times in the qualifying rounds of the 400-metre freestyle. She forgot the fact that her times in the American trials were faster than her Olympic effort. She conveniently forgot to mention that her time in Seoul eight years earlier was faster than Michelle Smith's winning time in Atlanta; faster to warrant questioning, if you were so inclined. After her dismal failure to qualify for the freestyle decider she elected not to swim in the consolation final, despite the fact that her coach urged her to compete in the 'B' final and prove her point by breaking the world record, medal or no medal. She refused. And she never did break that world record.

But she did break the world record for innuendo. Her suggestiveness was to dominate the headlines in the American press that Tuesday. 'I've heard a lot of things from a lot of various sources,' said Evans when she had taken the unprecedented step of calling a news conference directly after her unsuccessful heat. 'No. I've heard from a lot of people. It is a topic of conversation on the pool deck.'

'It' was the improvement in Michelle Smith's times. Evans, like a lot of Americans, didn't see beyond the tip of her nose or the Statue of Liberty when it came to sports observation. Michelle's European gold medals, her time at Pine Crest, her gradual improvement counted for nothing – purely because America hadn't sat up and taken notice until she had beaten one of their own at her own game. American journalists went against one of the principles of their profession. They began to ask the questions that had to be asked, but with pre-supposed opinions as to the answers on the few occasions that they bothered to pay any attention to Michelle Smith's replies.

Evans had said pre-Atlanta that she was looking forward to retiring from the sport, her sport: 'I just can't take smelling like chlorine anymore.' By the end of the Centennial Olympics she didn't smell of chlorine anymore. She did stink though. Just as much as her attitude did. 'She behaved as well as she swam – badly.' That was the description of Evans by the top American sportswriter Mike Lupica, days after she had followed her accusations against Smith by belly-flopping in the 800-metre freestyle, a performance that pointed the finger firmly back in the direction of one Janet Evans. But by then, it was too late: Michelle Smith had been more sinned against than she had sinned. By Tuesday she was getting used to the role of being America's public enemy number one. All America wanted was a piece of this action. NBC, ABC, CNN: the TV corporations scoured Olympic City, USA for more on the Evans case. After the glory of her second gold medal, Michelle was put on the rack again at the post-race press conference. Her replies were to dominate Tuesday's news as America came to grips with the fact that good old Evans had fallen from grace with a bang. The all-American heroine had won the 400-metre freestyle eight years earlier at the Seoul Olympics, in a world record time of 4:03.75; she had taken the silver medal at Barcelona. Yet, she had failed to make the final in Atlanta. Was this all because of Michelle Smith?

Michelle recalls: 'I was quizzed again on the Tuesday by the American press. They had had a sniff of a story and they were hot on the trail. Ireland wasn't supposed to breed swimming champions, so they latched onto the story. I just told them that I had been repeatedly tested in different places – at home in Holland, in Ireland, in competition abroad. For every American swimmer tested I had been tested five times. The FINA testing man even came to my door in Holland one Sunday morning when I was in my pyjamas. He was back two weeks later for another test.

'As I told the press conferences, it did not worry me because I had nothing to hide. I also told them that it was a great feeling to beat people who are really considered great in this sport. I told the American press I could understand their questioning. It was their attitude, their preconception that I had a problem with.

'My achievements only proved what can be done through hard work and dedication. Over the last couple of years, I had done nothing but eat, sleep and train for swimming six hours a day, six days a week. They found that hard to accept. They found it hard to accept that Erik had revolutionised my training programme. He had taken one look at my schedule in Ireland three years earlier and knew that I was wasting my time. So he took the best principles of athletics training and adapted it for the pool. At 23 years of age, I started to train properly for the first time in my life. It was hard. It was tough. It hurt. But it worked. I told them that some of them should try it some time. "It is very hard work," I told them.

'I also told them that it was downright stupid to take drugs. I've said that many times in the past. I have never used drugs, I have never been tempted. It would be really stupid once you are in the top 20 and subject to regular testing. Still the questions came. And one guy asked me to answer "yes" or "no" if I had ever taken performance-enhancing drugs. I told him the truth: "No, I haven't." I explained why: why it was wrong; why it would have been stupid. I'm not sure he listened to my answer. I'm not sure he wanted to. The answer didn't suit the story. They ignored the fact that testing in swimming is widespread now. Personally, I had undergone three tests in the three months before the Olympics. I must have been the most tested swimmer in Irish sport.

'I didn't know Janet Evans had made those comments until the press told me about them. After the heats, it was Sharon Davies of the BBC who told me that Evans hadn't qualified for the final. I knew then that the proverbials would hit the fan but I wasn't aware of Evans's comments. Because I had qualified for the final, I was resting when she took the unusual step of calling a press conference. I wasn't there; I didn't hear what she said until much later; I didn't even see her on the television. It was only at the post-final press conference on the Monday night that I discovered what she had said, when the journalists started to ask me about her remarks.

'I was very disappointed. Even 24 hours later I was still disappointed by her comments. I had always considered her a great swimmer and a great athlete; a good gal. Those were not the actions of a great

Michelle congratulating bronze winner Kirsten Vlieghuis (Holland) after the 400m Freestyle final.

In action in the 200m Butterfly at Atlanta.

Meeting President Clinton after winning her third gold medal. Erik is in the background in the bottom photograph.

Homecoming in Rathcoole, August 1996. *Left to right:* Michelle, Kathy
Stapleton (manager), David Hoffman (assistant).

ABOVE: Michelle shows off her medals at the airport.

OPPOSITE: The return home to Dublin airport where Michelle was met by President Robinson.

The homecoming.
ABOVE: On the bus to O'Connell Street.
RIGHT: On the way to Rathcoole.

Michelle is proud to be a fluent Irish speaker and it is appropriate that her
sponsor is Bord na Gaeilge.

champion. 'I said publicly that I'd like to remind her that in 1988 she had won the same two events as I had in times that were much faster than mine. In fact, her 400-metre freestyle time was unbelievable, a time she has never gone close to again. Maybe that should be scrutinised someday?

'I wasn't going to let it worry me, despite all the hype, all the nonsense. I still had two races to swim, two events to focus on. I can't stop people from making accusations, even stupid and false accusations. What it did do was to make me more determined. I'm a fighter when it comes down to it. When they put obstacles in my way, it just makes me more determined. This was the culmination of all my hard work and training regime. I wasn't going to let any of this take from it.'

Back in Ireland, the nation reacted angrily to the hysteria built up by Evans and the American media. Newspaper offices across Dublin took calls berating the American criticism of Ireland's gold medal heroine. RTE radio's phone-in shows were jammed with angry listeners condemning American jealousy and pettiness. The American embassy was subjected to a stream of phone calls from Irish citizens amazed and upset by the comments coming back from Atlanta. The Irish Olympic Council president, Pat Hickey, told the American media to grow up. 'They are just jealous that a little country like Ireland took the gold medal off them. I am astounded by the remarks.'

The Olympic Council of Ireland secretary, Dermot Sherlock, also lashed out at the criticism. 'The claims were nothing more than supposition and rumour. It was disgraceful that, having twice lost their appeals, the Americans then turned their focus to drug-taking. Michelle has been tested on at least six occasions already in Ireland. She was randomly tested walking out of a studio at the national television station without any prior knowledge whatsoever by an Olympic Council medical doctor.

'Unfortunately the American media seem to have to pass on things that have no substance or fact. The fact that her coach, Erik de Bruin, was banned is a different thing altogether from accusing her of taking drugs. The Americans were bad sports when they appealed against her entry to the 400-metre freestyle. I was very concerned about their subsequent allegations.'

Michelle's father, Brian, was subjected to the whole side-show in

Atlanta. He was chased by the American media almost as doggedly as his daughter was. When the US camera crews and recorders caught up with him, he told them: 'Janet Evans should be ashamed of herself. The whole American attitude and their innuendoes and remarks were a disgrace. We knew Michelle was clean but those people were dirty. The Olympics are all about spirit, however they were most unsporting.'

Back in Dublin, Lord Mayor Brendan Lynch was already beginning to plan the homecoming. 'The people of Dublin will be out in force to welcome Michelle home,' said Lynch. 'They realise she hasn't got as much out of swimming as other people have got from other events. She hasn't made as much money as some of the track athletes and yet she has achieved a huge amount. She's the first Irish swimmer to win at the Olympics and the first Irish woman to win gold.

'The original plan was to hold something in the Mansion House for the whole team; but after all the interest in Michelle, I can't see Dawson Street catering for all the people who will come to town. I think we could be looking at College Green now. I'd love to see something big, something befitting her achievements. It's a great moment for Irish sport.'

The Irish team in Atlanta also praised the girl from Rathcoole. Revealed 10,000-metre walker Deirdre Gallagher: 'We sat around a massive bank of television sets and cheered Michelle all the way home. It was so great for females in sport in Ireland. It was a very moving experience watching the final with the other members of the Irish team. I felt totally inspired and proud to be in the camp at that time. I didn't meet Michelle until I came out here to the Olympics but I quickly learnt of her hard work and dedication. She has been an inspiration to us all.'

The director of track and field coaching for the Irish squad, Jim Kilty, said: 'We cannot compete with the big guns around the world on a regular basis; but thanks to Michelle, we are on top of the Olympic world right now. We have got to suck in the moment and enjoy it. We do not win gold very often, so we must focus on the scale of the achievement and appreciate the tremendous hard work that went into this gold medal from both Michelle and Erik.'

Michelle's sister, Sarah, also jumped to her defence, the day before she was flown out to Atlanta with Aisling and brother Brian. Sarah told Brenda Donoghue on the great Gerry Ryan radio show: 'Evans doesn't know what she's talking about. If she knew Michelle she'd know that she doesn't drink, smoke, or even stay out late. All Michelle does is swim and train for swimming with Erik. It sounds like a very bitter Janet Evans to me. She's probably upset that she was ruled out of a medal chance herself because she didn't make the final.

'The allegations will not detract from our celebrations. You'll always get someone who will try to question the winner and try to spoil someone else's happiness. We've heard it before. She won't take anything from what Michelle has achieved and will achieve in the remaining days.'

Michelle Smith struck a great blow for Irish women, Mna na hEireann, in Atlanta. The country's leading lady, President Mary Robinson, paid her own tribute. She wrote to Michelle for the second time in 48 hours that Tuesday. Her letter read: 'We were still celebrating your first Olympic gold medal when you had the taste for more. In winning a second medal and again establishing a new national record, you have added a fresh chapter to Irish sporting history.'

On the other side of the Atlantic, the dirt-diggers were hard at work, but without always getting the answers they bargained for. When the Irish swimming team trained at Broward County in Florida for the first 17 days of July, Michelle and Erik had met Dr Samuel Freas, President of the International Swimming Hall of Fame. He had helped them to get pool time at Pine Crest, and had spent many hours in their company as Michelle wound up her preparations for the Olympic games. Freas was, in his own words, 'amazed at the way de Bruin had changed the whole approach to coaching and training swimmers'. And he was stunned to discover that Michelle Smith was lifting weights two weeks before the start of competition in Atlanta. A fortnight later, before the competition had begun, he had said: 'She will be the darling of the Olympic games.' And his prophecy had come true.

As Janet Evans cast doubts concerning Michelle, Dr Samuel Freas, a world-renowned expert on swimming, was throwing bouquets in her direction. 'I don't think we should ever take Olympic moments away from anybody,' said Freas after Smith's second gold medal haul. 'Swimming can learn a lot from track. We need innovation in the sport. Track athletes can maintain a high standard all year long, while in swimming we peak just once a year. Why not change that?

'I was amazed when I watched Smith in Pine Crest. You know when someone is ready to swim. She was ready to be the darling of the games then, and she was. This man, de Bruin, is very bright and looks at things differently.'

Still the American press tried everything they could to discredit Ireland's gold medal heroine. They scoured the stands at the Olympic pool for anyone with a Michelle Smith story to tell a nation stunned by the collapse of the Janet Evans legend. They found Deryk Snelling, a Canadian assistant coach at a club in Calgary where Smith had trained prior to Seoul and Barcelona. Snelling did not provide the incriminating answers the Americans wanted.

'I've worked with her enough to know that she could have done those times properly. One of the biggest factors in her success is her training and hard work, and I know all about that from experience,' said Snelling. 'The other factor is her mental toughness. When Michelle Smith is sick, she swims well. When she is injured, she swims well. When things are difficult, she swims well. You cannot take that away from her.

'The times in Atlanta were not very fast. A lot of people didn't swim to their potential. The Olympics puts a lot of pressure on people. It either takes you up or it takes you into trouble. With Michelle Smith, it took her up.'

It was to take her up again. Away from the hype that Tuesday night, Michelle Smith had already turned her attentions to the 200-metre individual medley as the countdown to Wednesday's heats began in earnest.

Then a problem developed. Michelle explains: 'The night before the 200-metre individual medley, I was in the shower, washing my hair when I turned and twisted my shoulder. I either pulled or strained something in my back and it was quite painful. Immediately I was afraid for the competition the next day, as I had to rotate my arms around in the butterfly. That was pretty sore to attempt on the Tuesday night. I had no idea how it was going to be the next morning.

'I asked the team doctor to look at it straightaway and he diagnosed it as either a slight tear or a slight strain. No decision could be taken on it until the next morning, so we decided to see how it was in the warm-up. If there was even a slight chance that I could pull or tear it further, then I wouldn't swim at all on the Wednesday.'

Atlanta Diary

WEDNESDAY, 24 JULY

Ireland had never won three Olympic gold medals before. It was beyond the wildest dreams of a nation born to the ideal that taking part *is* more important than winning. Sure, Bob Tisdall, Dr Pat O'Callaghan, Ronnie Delaney and Michael Carruth had all taken that a step further before Michelle Smith had first entered the waters of Georgia. But then they had been exceptions to the rule.

One gold medal was a cause for national celebration. Two gold medals were a cause for national elation. Three gold medals? Never! But headlines spoke of such an Olympic feat on the morning of 24 July. Few believed them. Few gave more credence than a nod of approval and a token of desire. It was great if it had happened. But if it didn't, they'd still serenade the Smith girl and her two gold medals, which were achievement enough in their own right for any Irish Olympian.

Michelle Smith didn't think like the rest of us though. She fancied her chances in the 200-metre individual medley, an event that had always borne the hallmark of approval in the Smith-de Bruin household. If her shoulder was up to it, she would be able to afford to go for it. The 200-metre butterfly, scheduled for the following Friday, 48 hours later, was the favoured event. As long as she was up to the 200-metres individual medley, she knew there was an outside chance. A nation hoped she could take the gold. She knew that it was worth a try.

Wednesday began well for Michelle Smith. Her injured shoulder had been well rested. The early morning ache and pain were certainly not a deterrent; they constituted little more than an irritant. She awoke with the relentless pursuit of a medal at the top of her agenda for the day, the day which was to be her third in the Olympic pool at the Georgia Tech aquatic centre.

Michelle recalls: 'That morning, we did a lot of talking when we got up. Because of the injury to my shoulder, I needed to be certain that I would be up to the demands of a heat and a race that day. I also needed to be sure that if I was to swim the 200-metre individual medley and make the final, that I would still have enough in reserve to carry me over to the 200-metre butterfly on the Friday, my most favoured event at the Atlanta games. We did a lot of soul-searching, a lot of talking back and forward on the subject. Erik even spoke to the Belgian Olympic coach and to one of the Dutch coaches. They said that I would be mad not to go ahead and swim on the Wednesday.

'Finally we decided to go ahead with the heat on the Wednesday morning. If I swam a good heat and made the final I would know exactly where I stood with the injury and my entry for the 200-metre butterfly. If I swam the heat, made the final, and felt that the other times were so fast that they would take the best out of me before the butterfly, then I could always pull out of the individual medley final and wait for the Friday. I couldn't lose by going to the blocks for the heats that morning. If I then reckoned that I would only make fifth or sixth in the final, I would pull out. If I had a chance of winning a medal, then it would have been stupid to throw it away.'

Subconsciously Michelle must have known that the eyes of America would be upon her that morning also. It was two days since their loud-mouthed media had shouted down her glory; now America waited for Michelle Smith to fall flat on her gold medals. Their spiteful media had offered the bait before the event. Two Americans had held high hopes in the revenge stakes: one was Kristine Quance, who was highly rated by the partisan home crowd; the other was Alison Wagner, the silver medallist behind Michelle Smith in the 400-metre individual medley the previous Saturday night. That night, Alison Wagner had made a pledge to the American television audience that the Irish camp had noticed. She had made it before when Janet Evans had failed to qualify for the 400-metre freestyle final: she had vowed to avenge Smith's gold medal haul.

Michelle remembers: 'Wagner had categorically said that she was more determined to win the gold in the 200-metre individual medley. I still don't know if she had been whipped up into a gold medal frenzy by the American media after the Janet Evans debate or if she had had a game plan all of her own, an agenda of her own after losing the final of the 400-metre individual medley on the Saturday night. I hadn't paid any attention to the media before the race so I didn't know which was the greater motivation. I did hear on the grapevine that she had pledged to make amends for Evans though after the result on Monday. She had also riled me at the press conference after the Saturday race. She had said then that defeat over the 400 metres had only made her more determined to win the gold over the shorter distance. After she had said that in the press room, I thought to myself, "I'll show you".'

Michelle Smith almost blew the chance to show Wagner and the rest in the final of the 200-metre individual medley. Her heat, the fifth and penultimate heat of the event that Wednesday morning, was one of the tightest as she raced against Wagner and the Dutch girl, Minouche Smit, for a place in the eight-lane final. The plan was for Michelle to test her shoulder in the warm-up pool, to see how fast the heats were generally, and then to decide on the final – if she made it. She almost didn't. One fifteenth of a second slower, less than the time it takes to blink an eye, and Michelle Smith would have qualified for the 'B' final of the 200-metre individual medley at the Atlanta games instead. That's how close it was for the golden girl of Irish swimming, the golden girl of the centennial Olympics.

Michelle winced as she recalled: 'The morning session was almost a disaster. In the heats, I was with the Dutch girl Smit, a Swedish girl, and one American girl. Ominously, that was Wagner, who really inflamed American passion and partisan support as soon as she stood on the blocks. My race plan was to start strongly during the first 50 metres, to maintain a good pace for the next 100 metres and to get the hard work in there, and then to ease up in the final 50 metres if I could afford to. But while I was coming up to the wall in the last 50 metres, the other girls came charging up and we ended in a block of four with all of us touching the wall within hundredths of a second. It was nerve wracking. I ended up third in the heat – and there was still another heat to come.

'When I had touched the pad and the time had come up, I knew that it was going to be close. I had a fair idea even then that it would be touch and go for a place in the final. It would have been a disaster if I hadn't made it. The shoulder had felt better in the water than it had done outside. I had felt comfortable enough with the distance. And the general times were nothing to scare me. If I had missed the final after all that I would have been very angry with myself.'

She had almost missed it! Michelle qualified for the final of the 200-metre individual medley by 0.15 of a second – she was billeted in lane one of the final, and America and its suspicious minds dismissed the threat of the double Olympic winner. Wagner, they claimed, was on her way to a gold medal. Michelle Smith, who had been out on the wings, was no threat. Or so they thought.

But then they had concluded thus with good reason. After all, Michelle had done nothing in that heat to justify favouritism or anything like that. Her near-miss was by no means exceptional. The Chinese girl, Yanyan Wu, fastest in the world for the year, had failed to make the final. Wagner, as it was to transpire, had left her best form in the heat she had won. Thus, like so many other American failures in Atlanta, she was to discover very quickly that they didn't give out medals for the heats.

Michelle now says, 'Because I was the seventh fastest, or the second slowest, of the qualifiers, I was assigned to lane one. That actually suited me, strange as it may seem. The fastest girls, including Wagner, were in the centre lanes, which were far enough away from me so that they couldn't see me, far enough away that they couldn't distract me. I knew the best part of the race for me was going to be the first 100 metres and the last 50 metres. Out in lane one, the other girls would be unable to judge what I was up to in those crucial stages. They would also be unable to drag me in and to dictate the pace of the race to their liking rather than to mine. That suited me. The 200-metre individual medley is very much a sprint event. In the 400-metre individual medley, you pace yourself over each 100 metres of the four disciplines: the butterfly, the backstroke, the breaststroke and the freestyle. In the 200-metre individual medley, you have a 50-metre sprint in each stroke. That suited me on the night even though my distance work has always been stronger than my sprint work. My lane position helped because it meant that I didn't have time to look around and see what they were doing, just as they wouldn't be able to watch me. Swimming in lane one meant that I could concentrate on a strong opening in the first 100 metres over the butterfly and the backstroke, then working hard on the breaststroke, my weakest discipline, before going for broke in the freestyle.

'When I saw the times in the heats – nothing spectacular even though I almost didn't qualify – I knew that I would have a chance in the final. The best time the Chinese had managed was 2:12 in their Olympic trials. Wagner and Quance had turned in 2:13 times. I could possibly get down to a 2:13, but a 2:12 would be almost impossible for me. As it transpired, the times for the heats were slower than they were for the world rankings. Only one Chinese girl, Li Lin, qualified. Quance blew up in the heats and didn't make it at all, even though her time in the American trials is still faster than anything I have ever managed. The biggest threat was going to come from Wagner and the Canadian champion, Marianne Limpert, a girl I was well accustomed to as a pool rival. I felt strong enough and confident enough to compete in the final. And so I went for it.'

That's exactly what Michelle Smith did – she went for it with a vengeance! She put her fault in the heats down to experience and wiped it from her mind as she rested that afternoon; then she rose to the ritual of an Olympic final. Talk of the gold medal dominated her pre-race conversations with Erik. They turned the outside lane into an advantage as the rest of the world dismissed it as home to a past heroine. They talked themselves through the race of a lifetime, the race to a third gold medal. And it worked. Her race plan was to take the first 50 metres butterfly out as fast as possible, and to build up as big an advantage as she could achieve before the conceived weaker breaststroke leg.

And that's exactly what Michelle Smith did. She took off like a tornado once again, eating up the first 50 metres in a time of 28.75, nearly 0.5 of a second ahead of the field.

Lin and Wagner made their first move on the backstroke leg, and they all but caught her after 30 metres. But she was still holding on to the lead at the turn into the breaststroke, with her split time of 1:02.97 giving her a slight advantage of 0.3 of a second over Lin and Wagner. Li Lin, renowned as a breaststroker, made her move in the third 50 metres. She caught Michelle at 125 metres with Wagner and Limpert in hot pursuit. By the turn, Lin had taken over the mantle of race leader with Limpert second, and a fading Wagner third. Michelle Smith turned fourth in a time of 1:43.44.

But she was about to play her ace card: her front crawl that had devastated the field in the 400-metre individual medley final four days earlier. The final 50 metres of the Olympic final belonged to Michelle Smith. She had been the fourth to turn, but she finished the race first after an incredible split of 30.49 to take the gold in a time of 2:13.93, almost 1.3 seconds inside her Irish record.

The final 50 metres simply devastated the opposition, even outwitted the American TV cameramen who had failed to catch her making the break for home. The Irish audience saw her turn for home in fourth; the next time the cameras caught her, she was first with 25 metres to go. Nothing was going to deny Michelle Smith her third gold medal. The time was not fast, but it was fast enough. Limpert took the silver, and Li Lin the bronze. Wagner was no better than a has-been.

Michelle recalls with satisfaction: 'The race went according to plan. I had known that I could take the initiative over the first 50 metres. I had expected to do enough to stay in front after the first 100 metres. And I had known that they would catch me on the breaststroke. The crunch for me was going to come on the turn into the front crawl in the final 50 metres. I knew then that even if they were going to be within sight, I could still catch them and beat them. I knew that going into the tumbleturn.

'When I caught sight of them in the middle lanes on that turn I knew that I was fourth. And I knew that it was time for the race of my life – time to put my head down and race for the wall like never before. I had the strongest 50-metre front crawl of any of them. It was time to use it.

'Still, it was important not to look around, not even to consider where they were. I had to go for broke and go for it on my own. Even when I touched the wall, I didn't know that I had won it. It was only when the number one came up after my name, that I knew that I had done it. I had gone for gold and won. I had taken a third Olympic crown. It was an unbelievable feeling.'

Irish victory had again come at the expense of American loss. This time it was Wagner who had failed to take the gold for one of the biggest swimming nations in the world. Two people were not all that surprised. Those two people were Michelle Smith and Erik de Bruin.

Michelle says, 'When we arrived in the warm-up pool area just before the final, we went over to the same place to get changed into my swimsuit. Wagner was sitting there, in her swimsuit, on the steps with a towel wrapped around her. You don't do that before an

Olympic final. You get changed quickly, you do your warm-up, you get out, and you get dressed again quickly. You don't want to get cold. If I had looked at her face then, I would have known that she wasn't ready to swim an Olympic final.'

And Erik adds, 'Perhaps it was harder on the Americans because it was in their own country, but that's their problem. Michelle's gold medal time was slower than the times at their Olympic trials. I know some of the swimmers complained that the pool in Atlanta was half a degree cooler than regulation demanded. But that does not count as an excuse – and it doesn't explain why their trial times were faster than the time that won the Olympic gold medal.'

The American media again tormented Smith after her third gold medal. Again she was hounded on the allegations made by Janet Evans. Michelle sighs, 'It was like a scratched record by this stage. I was being asked the same questions over and over again. They were asking the questions without listening to the answers.

'I pointed out that Janet Evans had swum 4:04 when she had won gold at the Seoul Olympics and nobody had questioned her. If I had been on something, surely then I would have swum faster than my winning time of 4:07. I just had to laugh when people started to make those accusations. I explained to them that I had known what I had been about, that my success had been due to hard work and dedication both from Erik and from me. It was nothing more and nothing less.

'One American even asked: "Can you answer in one word, 'yes' or 'no', if you have ever taken any form of performance-enhancing drugs?" The Irish journalists expected me to walk out. Instead I looked him in the eye and answered "NO." And they couldn't get away from the fact that for every American girl tested once I was tested five times – always with negative results.

'They tried to make this big thing of the fact that I was from Ireland, from a country without a 50-metre pool, from a country with no swimming tradition. They tried to make a big thing of my success against all those things. I told them: "I'm very proud of who I am and where I come from." I never make excuses for coming from a small country.'

The Americans even asked again if she had feigned the rumoured shoulder injury; she just laughed. 'I just said "Not true." I even smirked sarcastically: "Injury? All I have is a rash from shaving. Does that count?" That drew a laugh at the press conference. I still had a race to go. I wasn't going to give an opponent an advantage. Actually, if anything, the injury worked to my benefit in the 200-metre individual medley final. It had felt fine in the warm-up pool, the best it had done all day. But the word had filtered out somehow that I was having a problem with the shoulder, so I turned it into an advantage. The Canadian coach, for example, asked me before the race if I was going to pull out of the final because of an injury. I think the Americans quite liked the idea of spreading rumours about a Michelle Smith injury. But truly, the only way I wouldn't have swum was if I thought the qualifying times were too fast. I didn't want to tire myself out which would have ruled me out of a medal hope in my strongest event, the 200-metre butterfly on the Friday.'

Erik continued: 'Really, all they did was to help us. If the other coaches had been telling their swimmers that Michelle was out with an injury, then there's no doubt they must also have been telling them that they themselves had a better chance in the final. So when she turned up in the call-room for the final, they must have panicked; their faces must have dropped.'

As soon as the third gold medal was safely on board, the messages of congratulation poured in from home and abroad. President Mary Robinson led the thanks from a grateful Irish nation.

She told Michelle in a handwritten message: 'You have disturbed our sleeping patterns but lifted our spirits. Your performances in Atlanta – both in and out of the pool – have made Irish people all over the world proud. A third gold medal is a remarkable achievement. We are immensely proud of you.'

Taoiseach John Bruton, leader of the coalition government, said: 'Michelle's achievements make her a great Olympic champion; but she has also proved herself a true ambassador in the dignified way in which she has conducted herself out of the water. We hold our breath and wonder what further feats of sporting brilliance our triple gold hero can achieve. We know her three gold medals are rich reward for years of painstaking dedication, hard work and sacrifice. She is a great inspiration to us all.'

Michelle's former Irish team-mate, Gary O'Toole, a silver medallist at the European Championships in Bonn in 1989, had captivated the nation with his uncanny predictions on RTE television as Michelle was swimming her way into the history books. After the third gold medal, he too hailed her genius. 'Michelle Smith will be a legend: she will be a part of Olympic folklore,' predicted O'Toole after her victory in the 200-metre individual medley. 'When people talk about these Olympics around the world, they will talk about Michelle Smith. When you think that Ireland doesn't have a 50-metre pool and when you think of the facilities the others have had, it is a far better achievement than any other woman swimmer in history.'

Ominously, Sonia O'Sullivan had just touched down in Atlanta on the day of Michelle's third gold medal triumph. As she spoke to the Olympic press for the first time, she too was fulsome in her praise of the girl from Rathcoole. 'Michelle Smith has been an inspiration to all of us this week,' said Sonia. 'I just hope that I can live up to my side of the bargain now and win gold for Ireland and for Irish women as well. Michelle has been outstanding! It was incredible! I've never watched swimming before in my life, but I have been glued to it on the television for the last five days.'

That night, Michelle retreated to the sanctuary of the Olympic village again after the ritual press conference and drug test. She says, 'That's when I started to feel tired. I still thought I could keep going mentally, but physically it was a different challenge entirely. Going to bed that night, I knew that the next day when I got up, my legs would feel sore for the first time. I could have quit there and then and gone home more than happy with three gold medals.

'But I have never been a quitter, at any stage of my life. I had nothing to lose by swimming the butterfly. The heaviness in my legs was always going to be there until I finished. One more race wasn't going to make any difference physically or mentally. It was time to go on to the next race.'

That race was the 200-metre butterfly. And it did make a difference to the medal haul for Michelle Smith – and for Ireland.

Atlanta Diary

THURSDAY, 25 JULY

Not all Americans caught the Janet Evans bug. The morning after her third gold medal, Michelle Smith's face flashed across a thousand picture desks and across millions of television screens once again. This time it was to be for all the right reasons as far as middle America was concerned: the triple Olympic champion was to meet the President of the United States of America, some would say the most powerful man in the world – and almost the most powerful man in Olympic city.

Bill Clinton was due to attend the Olympics that day. He had done what a President had to do the previous Friday and helped to launch the greatest show on earth. On the following Thursday, he came back down to Georgia to lend a helping hand to Team USA.

The pool was a scheduled pit-stop on the Presidential diary for the day. He had a look poolside as the new American teen sensation, Brooke Bennett, swam in the heats of the women's 800-metre freestyle. He took in some gymnastics. He shook a few hands. And then he played the Irish card.

Ireland was important to Clinton. It has always been. Ireland in America equals votes – precious votes. He was seen by the powerful Irish–American community as the man who was to help in the bid to bring peace to Northern Ireland. He had visited Dublin and Belfast. He had said the right things, and he had been seen with the right people. He had been photographed in Cassidy's pub in the heart of working-class Dublin with the right pint of stout in his hand, depending on which Irish brewery you worked for.

When the Irish girl won a gold medal at the Atlanta games, Bill's spin-doctors sensed a good opportunity. When she won a second gold, they sensed a great opportunity. When America bit the hands that once fed it and built it, they sensed a wrong waiting to be set right by the great man himself. When Michelle Smith won her third gold the Presidential photo call was assured. Bill Clinton wanted to meet Michelle Smith. He wanted to congratulate her. He wanted to thank her. He wanted to tell her to ignore the American press, the same press that had made his life almost unbearable.

They met. It was on the Thursday, a non-event day for Michelle, sandwiched between the 200-metre individual medley and the 200-metre butterfly. It was her rest day. And it was a photo-opportunity day.

Michelle describes the meeting: 'I was in bed resting on the Thursday afternoon, having my carefully planned sleep, when Erik came into the room, woke me up, and said, "Somebody wants to meet you." I asked, "Who?" – as you do. He replied: "Well his first name is Bill." I knew straightaway who he meant and I started laughing. I just blurted out, "Bill Clinton," and he nodded his head in the affirmative.

'I got out of bed for that! We gathered my gear for a training session, got down to the warm-up pool, and met all his people. They brought us upstairs to the stands at the Olympic pool to meet the President and to have my photograph taken with him.

'He was genuinely warm and genuinely friendly. I was impressed with him. He acknowledged what I had achieved during the week and said he had kept a close eye on it. He also said he liked the way I had handled the "crap" – his word not mine – that the press had thrown at me. He was very forthright about that. He said his family had been through the same mill and knew what I was being put through. He told me to keep my head up, to handle it just as I had done, and to enjoy the final race.

'In return I thanked him for his time and interest, and invited him back to Dublin. I also promised him a T-shirt for his daughter, Chelsea. I didn't have one with me at the time, but I did promise to send one on to the White House. I must keep that promise!'

That photograph helped to set right the wrong that had been done to Michelle Smith. It restored the sporting image of America in the eyes of the Irish public. It did the President no harm. Ordinary Americans stopped Michelle and told her to ignore the criticism, almost apologising for the nonsense that had come her way. The Irish public agreed.

By Thursday, the letters from home had started to arrive at the Irish section of the Olympic village for Michelle. E-mail, telegrams and faxes had followed her first gold medal almost immediately, some offering congratulations, some offering advice, some offering true love and happiness to a woman who already knew the meaning of such words – and who was already very happy with the man who provided it. Then the letters arrived from Ireland, some simply addressed 'Michelle Smith, Atlanta'. It was then that Michelle Smith realised the fervour, the passion for sport and for swimming that she had whipped up back home.

'The hype had really started to build-up before the butterfly. But it was only when the letters came pouring in that I think I began to realise the effect the races were having on the people back home in Ireland. It felt good to see those people take the time and the effort to put pen to paper and to say, "well done".'

'There were a few drawings from children staying in hospitals in Ireland and they were really funny,' adds Erik. 'They had Michelle without any eyes or nose, just a big head with all this hair and "IRELAND" on her forehead!'

'I'm not sure I found that as funny as Erik did,' says Michelle, 'but it was great to see that support. I literally got thousands of messages afterwards – telegrams and all sorts. I even got one from a mental hospital. They were mostly addressed, "The Irish Team, Athletes' Village, Atlanta", and they all got to me. I also got over 3,000 messages on the Internet; it took us about four hours to print them out in the village. They were from people from all over the world. I got everything in some shape or other – flowers, letters and telegrams.'

The messages of congratulations and support were not all Irish. Some were from famous Americans, very famous Americans.

'I actually got a letter, which I still carry in my handbag, from the wife of Johnny Weismuller, the great swimmer and the Tarzan actor. She said that she had watched all the events, and that she admired the way I had swum and my spirit, especially in the 200-metre individual medley when I came out like a real smoker, a real battler, in an outside lane and won. She told me that my country should be proud of me; that she was proud of me; and that her late husband would have been proud of my attitude. I didn't realise who the letter was from until I got to the bottom of it. She also sent me a signature-card from the '50s with her husband's autograph on it, which I will treasure.

'Another fax I received was from Bill Cosby, the American actor and comedian. He wrote a poem for me . . . something like, "My little Irish rose, the most wonderful swimmer that grows" . . . then signed it "with regards" from his family. It was a nice touch from a gentleman.'

As sections of American culture tried to rectify wrongs done to Michelle Smith, so the United States embassy in Dublin entered the row over drug allegations after a flood of calls to their office high-lighting Irish anger at Stateside attitudes. Ambassador Jean Kennedy-Smith issued a statement through her embassy which said: 'On behalf of all Americans I'd like to congratulate Michelle Smith on her extraordinary performance in Atlanta. She was the brightest star in the Olympic constellation. Her dedication and determination have made her a wonderful role model for all young Irish athletes in Ireland and around the world.'

Thousands of miles away in Georgia, the Olympic Council Of Ireland President, Pat Hickey, saw fit to defend his country's most productive Olympian when he told the *Boston Globe*: 'We're particularly pleased by the third gold medal because of all the flak that has come Michelle's way. We asked for the results of the doping control tests to be made public to wipe away all the innuendo, rumours and smears. They have nothing to report.'

Meanwhile, the 50-metre pool debate was raging hot and fast. Former Olympic swimmer Gary O'Toole captivated the watching nationwide television audience with his psychic powers of forecast and with the fervour of his belief in the need for the provision of a 50-metre national pool. Politicians, anxious to be seen as swimming the party line, issued statements in support at a time when votes were easy to acquire within a sporting context. John Treacy, twice world cross-country champion and a silver medallist in the marathon at the Los Angeles Olympics, was left to fight the official corner in his role as chairman of the government's task force into the future of Irish sport. His televised answer was not what the new Michelle Smith fan club wanted to hear.

'A week from now we are going to be immersed in Sonia

O'Sullivan and track and field. Will we then be asked to lay down a track in every town in the county?' asked Olympian Treacy on the national station the night after Michelle's superb 200-metre individual medley performance, the night before her bid for another gold in the 200-metre butterfly. 'We tend to get carried away on a wave of hysteria after these big successes. We have to look at the issue in the context of our overall budget for sport.'

In England the fact that Ireland had no 50-metre pool was seen as something of a joke. To be fair to the British media though, some of them did come down on the side of Michelle Smith in the face of her constant criticism in America. In the *Daily Mirror*, Anita Longsborough, one of Britain's respected swimming experts said: 'She's like a machine. She just never knows when to stop when she's training or competing.'

Deryk Snelling, the Canadian who once trained Michelle in Calgary and is the new British swimming supremo said: 'Michelle is clean. She is the hardest working swimmer I've ever known. She always has been.'

Other sportsmen agreed. Irish rugby captain, Niall Hogan, said: 'It's absolutely astounding what she has achieved. Words can't describe the manner in which she has won three gold medals for a country that has no tradition in swimming at that level. She has set new standards. Her dedication to hard work and her commitment to her goals serve as an inspiration to all those who take part in sport. She has demonstrated what is required to reach the pinnacle in professional sport and no matter what sporting field you pursue you can't but marvel at what she has achieved.'

The former Irish soccer captain, Kevin Moran, was also lavish in his praise. He said: 'I was up late for every one of Michelle's races. It's astonishing what she's doing. Even in England, the response to her achievements has been wonderful. It gives a great sense of pride to everyone who is Irish. What she has done as an individual goes way beyond anything we have ever achieved as a nation in team sports. It is better than the World Cup or the European Championships. I can say no more than that.'

The hype in the Irish media was also growing by the day. Journalists who normally regarded swimming as a cushy summer marking were spouting fins in their efforts to explain the Smith phenomenon. They tried to put perspective on her achievement.

They likened her, in their best Jimmy Magee imagery, to the great Kristin Otto of East Germany, winner of four individual gold medals at the Seoul Olympics with another two in the relay thrown in for good measure. They spoke of Michelle Smith in the same breath as Mark Spitz, the great American who had also won four individual gold medals in the pool. They built Michelle Smith up for Friday night fever.

And while they did so, she tried to put those three gold medals to the side and to get her head together for one last medal attempt. However, she did make time that Thursday to have her photograph taken for the Irish media – with the three gold medals – outside the warm-up pool. And she did talk briefly to the press about the state of play up until then.

'It felt great to pose for pictures in the Olympic village with those three gold medals, which were more than I had ever dreamed of,' says Michelle. 'When you get that far in just a few short days, it is difficult to take it all in. But I coped. That Thursday, I was just looking forward to giving my all in the butterfly, followed by a good break, and a chance to relax.'

While Smith rested before her final assault on the gold-topped mountain, life carried on in the pool as her great rival, Egerszeggi, captured the 200-metre backstroke gold for the third games in succession to match Dawn Fraser of Australia in swimming's hall of fame. And like the rest of America that night President Clinton was enthralled with the performance of the 16-year-old Brooke Bennett in the 800-metre freestyle. She won the blue riband of distance swimming; she beat a top class field. And, like Michelle Smith, she left a certain Janet Evans trailing in her wake.

Michelle says: 'I think Evans swam so badly in the 800-metre final that she had little come-back on her previous statements. People wondered why she was making such a big fuss about me when she could only manage sixth in the heats for the 800-metre freestyle and no better as Bennett won the final. Evans's argument didn't hold much water after that performance.'

But Evans, the former cover girl of American swimming, of course neglected to mention that fact as she took her toe out of the water for the final time and immediately looked towards the business world that had devalued her Olympic bid.

'In the lead-up to Atlanta, Evans was half business woman and half swimmer,' says Erik. 'By being a jack of all trades and master of none, you cannot win gold medals at an Olympic games. Ever since Barcelona, Evans had done a lot of motivational speeches for corporate businesses in the States and made public appearances across the world. She loves that; and she refused to give that up prior to Atlanta.

'Before the games started, we read an interview with her coach which suggested that sometimes she skipped training sessions, that she didn't do as much pre-Atlanta as she had done for other Olympic games. I knew then that, if that was the case, she was out of the running as far as challenging for medals in Atlanta was concerned.'

'Somehow,' remarks Michelle, 'I don't think she will be asking me for a motivational speech!'

But stranger things have happened. Well, maybe not quite that strange!

Atlanta Diary

FRIDAY, 26 JULY

Michelle Smith sold sports papers and newspapers for a glorious week in the summer of 1996. Everything her face touched turned to gold as far as the media proprietors of Dublin were concerned. On the morning of Friday, 26 July, she sold more newsprint than ever. This was the day when Ireland would bear witness to the genius of the greatest sportswoman the country had ever produced. A country that barely knew the deep end from the shallow end talked with knowledge and passion about swimming – and about Michelle Smith.

A nation learnt the script and recited it. Butterfly is the favoured dance; backstroke the older cousin who has to be tolerated; breaststroke the big improvement; freestyle the forte. From gold on Saturday, gold on Monday, gold on Wednesday, a nation had watched and learned. This was their girl. This was their heroine.

The begrudgers could have their day. The Americans could try to taint their love for this heroine. But who cared? When the lights had come up, the cameras had rolled, and the frog had cleared from Jim Sherwin's voice, a people cared not for grudges or scepticism; a nation cared for just one thing: the scent of the kill; the scent of victory; the colour of gold.

Friday dawned, the weekend started here. It would be another golden weekend, another Friday night in front of the big screen, glass in hand, toast at the ready. The Irish hoped and cheered. 'Olé, Olé, Olé.' Italia '90 revisited; USA '94 revisited; Croke Park; Lansdowne; Gothenborg. Limerick racecourse; Barcelona. They were all revisited A nation was gripped to the screen: to watch the green and the gold:

149

to watch a swimming race. The face of Irish sport had changed: a nation passionate about its sport now had a new heroine – and a new medal in its sights.

The expectation was great; comparisons were sought; comparisons were given. Names from the history books were bandied about in comparison: great names; great champions; great swimmers. They talked about great Olympic feats: like those of the legendary Mark Spitz who had won a record individual haul of four golds in individual events at Munich in 1972 to which he added three more in the relays. Like those of the East German, Kristin Otto, who had also won four individual golds and two more in the relays at the 1988 Seoul Olympics when Michelle Smith was just taking her first steps on the world ladder. On the track, many had been invited, but few had reached such heights. In 1936, a man by the name of Jesse Owens went to the heart of Nazi Germany and won four gold medals on the track. Then Carl Lewis went to Seoul 52 years later and repeated the heroics of his great idol. He had done that with the backing of the world; but Michelle Smith was now attempting to do it with only the backing of her own people.

Michelle says, 'I was lucky that I was closeted away in Atlanta at that stage. I knew from talking to my parents and my sisters and brother Brian that there was great craic at home, great expectation. But in the comfort zone of the Olympic village, I had only the daily presence of the media at the pool to remind me of the pressure I was under. As far as I was concerned, any pressure I had was going to be self-made. I wanted to get in that pool and win a fourth gold. I wanted to forget about the weariness that was developing in my legs and arms. I wanted to dismiss the shortening stroke that was develop-ing in the warm-up pool, a natural reaction to the demands of three Olympic finals in six days. My only wish was to swim the final of the 200-metre butterfly, and bring the curtain down on my Olympic games with another medal. And then I wanted to relax.'

No one said it was going to be easy, not even the bar-stool experts now applying to *Mastermind* with Olympic swimming as their specialist subject. The competition was tough. The Australian, Susan O'Neill, had arrived in Atlanta with a time of 2:07.29 under her belt, less than a second down on the Olympic record of 2:06.90 set by the American, Mary Meagher, at Los Angeles in 1984. O'Neill was renowned as a sprinter with a kick like a mule. If Michelle Smith was to be within her grasp at the final turn, then there would be a real danger to the Irish party. She was not the only threat. Japan's Hitomi Kashima, fourth in the 100-metre butterfly, had recorded a time of 2:08.69 prior to Atlanta. The Chinese girls, Liu and Yun Qu, were both fast over the shorter distance, well capable of pacy times.

Smith's Irish record had been 2:11.60, the seventh fastest in the world going to Atlanta. Another Herculean effort would now have to be called for in order to win the gold that would ascend Michelle Smith into the halls of Olympic legend. The fact that Michelle had raced 2,200 metres before the final event – and won three gold medals in the process – was also a cause for concern. But it was only a mere distraction from the job in hand. The buzz word once again was 'gold'.

The day began well. A message arrived in Atlanta from the Irish government leader, John Bruton. It read: 'The tricolour has flown high with pride in Atlanta. I hope to see it raised again tonight.' His remarks echoed the best wishes of a country happily resigned to another late-night celebration thanks to a sport that had captured the imagination of a willing nation.

The International Olympic Committee too came out in Smith's favour that morning. They had been alarmed at the outbreak of innuendo that had gripped Atlanta in the wake of her three gold medals, the virus that had spread through the American media. They had had no evidence to back up the media claims, no evidence against Smith or any swimmer in the Atlanta pool. They now sought to put the record straight – and to put some perspective back in the coverage of their sport.

That morning, IOC spokeswoman, Michelle Verdier, called a press conference at the Olympic village. She told the world media: 'I warn people not to use the name of an athlete along with unsubstantiated allegations and rumours. Besides being an athlete she is a human being and she has the rights of a human being. Simply throwing a name around when nothing is proved is very wrong and very unfair on the athlete. When the Medical Commission tells us there is something wrong, we will release the results from doping control. When there is nothing wrong, there is no release. There is nothing to report from any doping test.'

That was almost enough to quell the doubters; almost. But back in the pool, the competition was all that mattered. The morning heats saw Michelle easing into the Olympic final. She broke her Irish record by over a second, coming home in 2:10. A nation waited with bated breadth.

Michelle says, 'There was a lot of debate before the heats in the swimming camp as to the validity of trying for another gold medal; but I myself was confident enough. The butterfly has always been one of my strongest disciplines, and we had worked too hard in the past at it for us to forsake it now on the final day of competition in the pool. With hindsight, it is easy to say that I was too tired after the efforts of the week to win a fourth gold medal; but I have never been one for hindsight.

'The heats went okay. I swam 2:10 but my stroke was getting short on the final 50 metres. I was getting tired at that stage, but I also felt that I could shrug it off for one more race, one more effort. The time was a personal best, good enough to suggest that I could do better with only 200 metres left of Olympic competition. If anything, I felt that I could trim another two seconds off it, since in the Olympic pool up until then the times had rarely been earth-shattering. Yes, that might well have been enough.'

Michelle Smith did improve on her time in the Olympic final; she did beat her Irish record by a second. But she did not win the gold; and the main reason for that was a piece of fishing line and a pair of goggles. In the call-room before the final of the 200-metre butterfly, Michelle Smith's goggles snapped. They were the goggles which she had worn at the World Championships in Rome in 1994 when she had finished fifth in the 200-metre butterfly and with which she had won the 400-metre individual medley 'B' final. They were the goggles which she had worn for two golds and a silver at the European Championships in Vienna in 1995. And they were the goggles which she had worn for three Olympic finals and three Olympic golds in Atlanta. Now they had snapped – and they were to tear at her medal prospects.

Michelle says, 'The incident with my goggles is not an excuse. It never will be, but it did put me off. It unsettled me at a time when routine and habit are everything in the minutes before a big race. I had a ritual preparation and it was thrown into disarray. That did not help.

'I was standing in the call-room with my goggles in my hand when all of a sudden they snapped. Normally that would not have been a problem. I carry a few pairs of goggles in my gear bag at all times when I am competing. Although the bag wasn't with me in the call-room, it was outside with Erik. So there shouldn't have been a problem. All I had to do was to tell the officials that I had a problem with my kit, and they would have allowed me to go out to Erik and get another pair. Under the rules, if you have a problem and inform an official about it, he or she has to hold the race for you.

'But when I went to the corridor, there was no sign of Erik. For the first time at the Olympics, he was not there; he was not in the area immediately outside the call-room . So I went back to the race referee and told him I had had a problem with my equipment. I asked another official I knew to find Erik for me. I asked the referee to hold the race as I was entitled to under the official guidelines for an Olympic final.

'The official searched the warm-up pool for Erik and couldn't find him either. Then a guy popped his head out of the call-room into the corridor and told me that the swimmers were on their way out to the bank at the poolside for the introduction before the 200-metre butterfly final. I was caught in a no-man's land. I was standing there with no goggles and an Olympic final about to start without me. There was a Dutch girl, Marianne Muis, in the warm-up area preparing for the next final. I rushed up to her and asked to borrow her goggles. She agreed, and I rushed to the pool, well behind the other finalists.

By this time, my concentration was gone. It may sound funny to non-swimmers, but goggles are a precious item. They are personal and individual. You have a pair that is shaped to your face, a pair that keeps the water out when you dive into the pool. I had gone to the call-room with the same pair that I had worn for my gold medals; but now I was standing on the blocks with a pair belonging to somebody else, a pair that was far too big for my face. I tried to forget about it. I tried to put it to the back of my mind, to get my concentration back for the race – but it was difficult. It had all happened too fast and too close to the final.

'The fact that they had been prepared to start an Olympic final without me, in contravention of the rules, upset me. It threw me off guard. The race was never right for me after that incident; but that is not to suggest for one minute that I would have won gold with my own goggles. Silver maybe, but not gold definitely.'

Erik says, 'I had watched all Michelle's previous finals in that corridor area below the pool and beside the call-room. Because it was the last day and Michelle's final race I decided to take one of the seats in the stand that were only available to the swimmers and the coaches if they had not been sold out to the spectators. It was the first time I had done that all week – unfortunately.

'When the swimmers came out for the parade and Michelle was missing, I knew that there was something wrong. Then she came out with these saucers on her little face instead of goggles. Just before the gun went, she was still fiddling with the goggles, trying to fix them. I knew they weren't hers. And I knew they wouldn't help her in the race itself. I knew something was wrong but I was helpless. There was nothing I could do, sitting high in the stand.'

The incident did affect Michelle Smith. The timing of the 200-metre butterfly final also affected Michelle. If the race had been swum at the start of the week, she would have been fitter and fresher. Instead, the final proved just one thing: Michelle Smith was human after all.

She did not begin well. She was not herself for the first 100 metres – and it made all the difference. The final was the first of the four she competed in that did not go to plan. As Gary O'Toole told the nation on RTE television, she had needed to get off to a fast start, to lead the field at the first 50-metre turn. But for the first time in her finals, she was not to the front at that first turn. Susan O'Neill set the early pace and led Michelle into that tumble turn. The Irish girl's split was a respectable 29:16; it was fast, but not fast enough. O'Neill now took inspiration from her lead against this superwoman, against a woman she later admitted she had been frightened of prior to the start of the butterfly final. By the 100-metre mark, O'Neill was still to the front, half a second ahead of Michelle Smith's 1:01.30 split.

The third 50 metres was to be the platform for Michelle Smith's kick. However, when she put the foot down, there was nothing there; the week was taking its toll. Instead, it was the Australian champion who kicked for home. Her compatriot, Petria Thomas, in lane three, kicked as well. Now Michelle Smith had an Olympic fight on her hands. Somehow she summoned more energy; somehow she dug into the bank of resolve and came out fighting. As Thomas made her charge in the final 50 metres, Michelle Smith dug deep. She was caught, but only in the final metre by Thomas. She held off the rest. Victory was not hers; the bronze medal her consolation for that last gargantuan effort – and a new Irish record in a time of 2:09.91.

Michelle recalls: 'I never led the final at any stage; that's where it was won and lost. I needed a big start and I never got it, largely due to the fact that I was suffering from fatigue, partly due to the fact that the goggles had snapped under the rigours of the Atlanta heat and humidity. Throughout the race, I was caught between second and third. The Australian girl, Susan O'Neill, who won it is good, very good. She is a fitting Olympic champion who did her country proud in Atlanta. I knew going into the race that she was going to be one of the girls to beat. I was happy for her that she too sampled that gold medal experience. I was happy for myself that I had won the bronze. In the aftermath of three gold medals, some may have viewed that as a disappointment. Not me; how many times in the past would we have been happy to see an Irish swimmer reach an Olympic final, never mind winning a medal of any hue?

'In the end, I got very emotional for the first time in Atlanta. After the medal ceremony, I broke down and cried. When they put that final medal around my neck I suddenly felt like crying. It was strange because all I had ever felt on a presentation podium was nervousness. I was crying out of sheer happiness, crying because I had just had the best week of my life. I cried again afterwards, tears through happiness, through elation. The stress, the tension, the joy flooded through me when Erik put his arms around me after that prize-giving. Many people watching thought I was crying through disappointment. I wasn't; my tears were veiled only with pride.'

That night Michelle Smith and Erik de Bruin celebrated victory; they celebrated gold and bronze, with a slap up meal in an American-Irish bar. The Olympic champion, trained on a diet of lean meat, low-fat foods, chicken and pasta, dined on burgers and ribs. She raised a toast with her husband – her glass containing nothing stronger than the real thing.

Later that night a bomb exploded in Centennial Park as security fears surrounded the Olympic games. Michelle and Erik were down town in Atlanta when the bomb exploded. In the taxi, on the way back to the village, they met a fleet of ambulances, fire trucks and police cars *en route* to the scene.

Back in the safety of their room, Michelle slept soundly, the slumbers of an Olympic champion. A nation too went to bed, belatedly and happily. As the curtain came down on the swimming competitions in Atlanta, a nation force-fed on a diet of sporting defeats held its head high.

Atlanta Diary

SATURDAY, 27 JULY

The morning after the week before. The Olympics were over for Michelle Smith and Erik de Bruin. It was effectively over for Ireland, though no one could have known it at the time.

One girl from Rathcoole had surpassed anything that Bob Tisdall, Pat O'Callaghan, Ronnie Delaney and Michael Carruth had managed in their lifetimes. One girl from Dublin had taken Irish sport to a new level, to a new high. She had won three gold medals. She had won a bronze in her fourth final. She had smashed Irish records.

She had broken American hearts. She had behaved like the champion the Atlanta Olympics never deserved; a champion with dignity running through her veins in the face of American innuendo; a champion who answered their doubts, their cheap vulgar shots, with a charm to which they were not entitled. She had become one of the great Olympians of all time.

But now it was all over. She had graced our screens with her presence, our hearts with the magnitude of her achievement. And now it was all gone. The Olympic camera had new targets, new heroes: Michael Johnson; Carl Lewis; Donovan Bailey. Their time had come.

For drama in the pool, read trials and tribulations on the track and in the field. American television, apt to switch to advertising when Michelle Smith was beating their girls, found the sports where their heroes collected medals and not condemnations. Thus Ireland went into post-gold medal depression. After a week of late nights and flag-flying, the gas had run out on the emotional roller-coaster.

In Ireland, a nation raised one last salute to their heroine. In Atlanta, Michelle Smith and Erik de Bruin packed the aquablade suit away one last time and prepared to enjoy life in the fast lane of Olympic championship.

Michelle comments, 'I was tired and emotional on the Saturday. The emotion of the week had exploded in a sea of tears the night before. I had finally released the flood valves on the trauma, the pressure, the exhilaration. I cried my eyes out after the medal ceremony and it felt good. It felt really good.

'That had been the greatest week of my life and I was proud – so proud of what I had achieved – so proud that I had gone to Atlanta as a contender only in my own mind and Erik's, and left with three gold medals and a bronze. I had realised my potential and my dream. Four years of swimming, training and dedication had paid off in one magical week. It felt good to wake up that morning and count medals in my mind.

'There was the luxury of a lie-in until 8.30 a.m. even though my body started to wake up at 5 a.m. as usual – the luxury of not having to make a trip to the warm-up pool. It was the luxury of relaxation, the luxury of achievement. That all felt good that Saturday morning.

'What is it the Americans say? "Today is the first day of the rest of your life." It was true that Saturday morning; and I had so much to look forward to. There was the future in the pool, the new status of life as an Olympic champion, and the plaudits that would bring in the world of competition. There was the homecoming to look forward to; the chance to meet the people of Ireland, and to show them the medals that I was sure meant as much to them as they did to me. There was the future as man and wife with Erik, the honeymoon we had forsaken in the Olympic cause, the chance to plan for the future like all newly married couples.

'And all the time there was the comfort of those four Olympic medals.

'But there was an element of sadness too, a disappointment that the whole experience was coming to an end. I had enjoyed the competition; I had relished the races; I had thrilled to the challenge put down by Egerszeggi, Wagner and O'Neill. That too was gone; but the pleasure of victory more than made up for that feeling of emptiness.'

That afternoon was interview-time once again, America's last chance to talk to the golden girl who had stood Janet Evans, Kriztina Egerszeggi and Alison Wagner up. CNN, NBC, Larry King and Oprah Winfrey all battled for their pound of flesh with the rather more appealing tones of Sharon Davies from the BBC in London and George Hamilton from RTE in Dublin.

The questioning continued; but so did the dignity of the answers, the behaviour of the champion. They asked the questions. She provided the answers. She provided them with honesty and dignity – and a hint of doggedness.

Michelle says: 'They seemed surprised by my honesty and forthrightness. They shouldn't have been. This is a tough sport; only the strong will survive. If you want to be the world champion or Olympic champion, you have to be a fighter as well as a swimmer. I know that now. Four years ago – eight years ago – I would have caved in under the pressure of that challenge. But not now, not after four years of working my mind and body under Erik's guidance.

'I know my public image is that of a hard, tough woman, and I believe it does reflect me correctly. In competition, there has to be a hardness, a severity of approach. But there is a heart in there also. Just ask Erik!'

Erik agreed. 'The public don't see that side of Michelle when she's in competition. I don't think she should show her deepest feelings to the public in general; it is something that is private and it must be kept that way.'

Michelle: 'Yes. I have to be tough to succeed in swimming.'

Erik continued. 'When that comes across in competition, people assume that Michelle is like that all the time. It was the same perception that people had of me in Holland when I was competing at world level. There is a difference, even looking back on my own career, between doing interviews straight after a competition or doing one a couple of days later. During competitions, I was seen as being intense and cold. Later, if reporters were to meet me when I was having a cup of coffee, I could be relaxed, a different person. That is why people accused Michelle of being tough in Atlanta; it was because they only saw her immediately before or after competition, when she was totally concentrated. If anything, she was more focused – more stern if you like – in Atlanta because she had to be defensive with the very nature of the questions and allegations that were coming at her.'

Michelle: 'I came out fighting in the Atlanta press conferences because I had to. I wasn't going to sit back and let the American press tear me apart. Those type of questions were still keep coming from the American press on the day after my competition ended. They even came when I went back to America in the October following the Olympics. They will continue to fire those questions at me for the rest of my swimming career, for the rest of my public life. I wasn't going to run from the questions. I have nothing to hide. I gave as good as I got. I don't feel I should have to apologise for that.'

Erik explains: 'In America, Michelle is now in a no-win situation. They had formed an opinion of her towards the end of the first week and that will hold. They will not turn around and say, "Yes, she did swim really fast and maybe our swimmers just could not match her." They will not admit defeat.'

Michelle concurred: 'Even after the event, it was hard for the American coaches to admit that they had really failed with some of their swimmers out there. They couldn't stand up and admit to failure, so they started to throw stones in other directions.

'But all they really have to do is to examine the facts, both the American press and the American swimming community. Their swimmers swam really fast times at their Olympic trials, faster times than I swam to win my Olympic medals. Then, when it came to Atlanta, they couldn't do it. They couldn't transfer trial times into Olympic times and they were beaten on their own patch in front of their home crowd. They just couldn't accept that; which meant that the afternoon after my final race I was still being asked to explain myself to the American public, when all they had to do was to accept defeat. And maybe even acknowledge it.

'The interviewers always ended with the same question, "Would you come back to America?" I said "yes" every time. Despite what happened, what was said, what was insinuated, I will go back again. I have been back already post-Atlanta. I'll race in America again if I get the invitation. In fact, if Janet Evans wants to come out of retirement and take me on in the States, I'd consider it. The coaches couldn't accept but thankfully towards the end of the week public opinion was changing.

'I do intend to work out there. As I said on the final day of interviews in Atlanta, by that stage there had already been approaches from some American companies to undertake speaking tours in the

States. I told the interviewers that I would consider them. I have made speeches and addressed audiences before. I did some similar work with TNT last year. I haven't had much time in the past, but it is something I can do, something I will do. I don't mind standing up in front of people and talking. I use a script for the motivational speeches, but anywhere else I just ad-lib.'

Back home, Ireland was waking up to the end of the Michelle Smith experience. For the moment at least, all eyes were turning towards Sonia O'Sullivan and the athletes on the track. However, Ireland did wonder what might have happened over the 200-metre butterfly if Michelle had opted out of the 200-metre individual medley.

Michelle says now, 'When it was all over, a number of people asked me about the decision to swim in four events. In hindsight, it was a tall order with the races so close together. In hindsight, it is easy to say that it was a mistake but I don't accept that. I will however look at the race schedules at the next Olympics in Sydney and probably for the next European championships and World championships as well.

'But it was right for me in Atlanta. I believed that at the time, and I still believe it now. I knew I could swim the four races; I knew I could do well in the four events.

'Yes, I was tired by the time the butterfly came around on the Friday. And, yes, I did consider withdrawing from the 200-metre individual medley on the Wednesday; but the heats had convinced me that I had a chance of winning the medal. Those who suggest I deprived myself of a gold medal in the 200-metre butterfly by swimming the 200-metre individual medley can't understand how much that third gold medal meant to me, or how much the bronze medal on the Friday meant. I have no regrets.

'If the 200-metre butterfly had been at the start of the week, I may have swum a faster time, and I may have won it. Who knows? All I know is that I swam four races at the 1996 Olympic games in Atlanta, won three of them, and came third in the final one. Nobody can ever take that away from me, no matter how many "ifs" they enter into the equation.'

It was a measure of Michelle's earlier endeavours that her bronze medal was almost deemed a disappointment by many back home. RTE news spoke of her failure to win a fourth gold medal. A week earlier they would have deemed a bronze medal a fantastic achievement. You can't please everyone all the time.

One little boy put it all into perspective on a radio phone-in show that Saturday morning. He asked the presenter, 'How do you recognise an Irish woman in an American swimming pool?' The answer was obvious. 'She's the one with the gold medals around her neck.'

It had been that sort of week.

CHAPTER TWELVE

Home

The homecoming began in America amongst the Irish communities of Boston and New York, communities where their welcome served only to hint at the warmth and excitement to come back home in Dublin. Ireland as a nation is not touched too often by the success of its sporting heroes; thus the Irish people wanted to recognise Michelle Smith for what she was. First, though, the Irish people in America wanted to say 'thank you' for a job well done.

Michelle recalls: 'For the duration of the competition in Atlanta, we had been closeted away from the hype and the excitement back home. I had heard all the stories from home about the craic in the pubs and the pleasure everyone was taking from the swimming finals. My parents had shared that excitement with me. When Sarah, Aisling and Brian came out in the middle of the week they were able to relay the buzz as well. But it was only when I got out amongst the Irish in America that I realised how much the four medals had meant to other people, how much their joy reflected the happiness that success had brought to Erik and me.

'The welcome in both Boston and New York, when we did some promotional work for TNT, was phenomenal. We attended a reception at the Irish Consul in New York and I was mobbed by the Irish people there, both first and second generations. So many people rushing forward for signatures and photographs that Erik had to pull me out of the room. That brought home to me how much it meant to Irish-Americans to see one of their own land gold in Atlanta. It was then that I knew how much pride they had taken in the three gold medals and the bronze.'

After her quick flight north for those events in Boston and New York, Michelle went back to Atlanta, back to the Irish quarter for the remainder of the Olympics. As in Barcelona and Seoul, she was happy to indulge herself in the Olympic spirit, to be a part of the team, to cheer the other athletes on.

Like the rest of Ireland, their next gold medal hopes were pinned on Sonia O'Sullivan. Like the rest of Ireland, Michelle Smith felt only sorrow and pain when Sonia's Olympic dream collapsed around her: 'I think all of us in the Irish camp were stunned into disbelief by what happened to Sonia on the track. I don't think my success took away any of the pressure on her. She was expected to win the 5,000 metres because she was by far the favourite, the fastest in the world. I felt very sorry for her because I know how much work you have to put in to get that far.

'The Olympics only comes once every four years so if you fall ill or lose out you have to wait another four years for your chance. No matter what other competitions, medals or money you win, nothing compares to winning an Olympic medal. Sonia was unfortunate. Four years ago, she was fourth in Barcelona. This year she had this mishap in Atlanta. Now she has to wait another four years for another chance – and anything can happen in four years.'

Like all Ireland, Michelle Smith too was dismayed by the way Sonia was treated by Irish officialdom. On the day after her dramatic collapse in the 5,000-metre final, Sonia was wheeled out in front of the press. She answered questions for half an hour. She then sat through an incredible hour-long debate between the Irish Olympic Council and the country's athletics federation (BLE) as they washed their dirty linen in public.

The row was all over gear. BLE, the athletics body, had a sponsorship agreement with one company. The Olympic Council had a deal with another company. Sonia had to change her gear in the tunnel area only minutes before the heats of the 5,000 metres. The row over which gear she should have worn is still raging on. It dominated that press briefing. And Sonia was caught in the middle of it at a time when she should have been aided in her recovery from the trauma of her 5,000-metre final.

Michelle said: 'I didn't see Sonia's press conference but I was aware of the row over gear. The swimmers were in a similar situation over the gear issue. The Olympic team was sponsored by Reebok, and we got Reebok swimsuits going to Atlanta. But our association is sponsored by Speedo. In some cases, the swimming federations were insisting that the swimmers wear their gear rather than the gear of the Olympic Council's sponsors. As far as I am aware, a court case has arisen in New Zealand on that very subject.

'My view was that I wanted to wear the fastest swimsuit, the one I was most comfortable with. If one swimsuit makes the difference of one one-hundredth of a second, then it is worthwhile wearing it. Obviously, when you are in there, you want to give yourself the best chance. In the end we didn't have any major hassle over it. Thankfully.

'As I said, I didn't see the press conference after Sonia's race when the OCI and BLE had their public row, but I would not have stayed there anyhow. Erik would have taken me out of there. At that stage there was no point in staying; it was not a row she was involved in anyway. I probably wouldn't have gone to the press conference in the first place.

'In my case, Erik doesn't mind if he offends anybody or if people think he is rude. On occasions he has had to take me away from reporters when I have had to do a swim-down, or to have lunch or a rest. People might have said at those times that they had only needed five minutes more and that he was being rude. But Erik says he doesn't care, I am his top priority. We have put in so much work and effort that he's not going to let a press conference upset our rhythm.'

Michelle Smith never got a chance to offer Sonia any words of comfort. She does though have a message of support for the Cobh girl. And she believes Sonia O'Sullivan will bounce back with the style of a true champion.

Michelle says, 'I never saw Sonia at all in Atlanta. I think it is normal for her to stay by herself. I met her last year at the sports awards, but it was Barcelona before that. I think she will bounce back next year. She will start running well again, although it may take until next season before she recovers mentally. Next year there is the World Championships where she is reigning champion, and the year after it's the Europeans. She'll be back.'

While Sonia stayed away from the Olympic village and the team's homecoming party in Dublin, Michelle was the centre of attention. And she liked it.

The Irish team left for home on 6 August. They left a hot and humid Atlanta behind them. The next morning, their flight, delayed by over an hour, touched down in Dublin, a very wet and damp Dublin, a very happy and delirious Dublin. The rain kept the numbers down but not the spirit. Michelle Smith stood on the tarmac at Dublin Airport at 9.27 a.m. on Tuesday, 7 August.

Home was the heroine. She was greeted by President Mary Robinson. She was hailed by the Minister for Sport, Bernard Allen, and the people of Dublin and Ireland who braved the elements.

An open-top bus into the city centre followed. Michelle and Erik stood at the front out in the rain, out to wave and smile, and out to thank the well-wishers who had done their bit to acknowledge her achievement. She floated into O'Connell Street on a tidal wave of congratulations and rain. She didn't care.

The city fathers of Dublin donned their ceremonial robes for the official welcome outside the GPO in O'Connell Street. George, Paul, and Eddie Furey serenaded the crowd with their song 'Princess of the Tide', composed especially for the occasion by the former Eurovision songwriter, Teresa O'Donnell, from The Curragh.

Dublin's new Lord Mayor, Brendan Lynch, national marathon champion in the late '50s, spoke of the great day for Ireland, for all the women of Ireland. He thanked her for her effort and achievement in Atlanta. The thousands who had braved the elements echoed the sentiment. And all the while, Michelle Smith attempted to take it all in.

Michelle glows. 'The homecoming with the team was important to me. It had been a team effort and I was part of the team. I never saw myself as being different from anyone else. When I was finished in the pool, there were still other Irish team members competing. They are the same as I am; their moments are no less important to them than mine were to me.

'I wanted to be there with the team, to be part of the team. It was good to be around the Irish block. There was a constant camaraderie between the boxers and the swimmers just as there had been in Seoul and Barcelona. It was good fun.

'I had expected to be singled out at the homecoming, but I had no idea how many people were going to be at the airport. The television people had a crew on the plane and they even had a helicopter following the plane in on its approach to Dublin, filming it as it landed. I was sitting there thinking that this was like a different world. I was even upgraded on the plane coming home. I normally wouldn't do it but it was such a long flight that I felt I might as well sit in a bigger seat!

'My first thoughts getting off the plane were for the poor people standing in the rain with banners and flags, getting soaked for their efforts. When we had come home from Barcelona four years earlier, Wayne and Michael got off the front of the plane, and the rest of us got off the back and got in through normal arrivals. The two lads then went to a reception, but the rest of us were down in the public area, waiting for our bags and our families like everyone else.

'This time it was different. I was singled out for special treatment. I was interviewed on the tarmac. I was given the Presidential welcome, I was escorted through the VIP area and onto the open-top bus for a journey into the centre of Dublin that was both wet and fun.

'There were people coming out of offices and shops waving at us so I didn't mind standing up there getting wet. If those people could take the time and make the effort to come out and welcome me home, then I could make the effort to stand out in the rain and accept their greetings. O'Connell Street was great. So many people came out in the rain to welcome me home. Their warmth was incredible.'

The real homecoming came that night as the village of Rathcoole came out to greet one of their own, the population of the Dublin suburb swelled by an influx of well-wishers from all over Ireland. Even the country singer, Daniel O'Donnell, joined the party as the Smith family welcomed him with their gold medal daughter at the top of the open-top bus as it wound its way down the dual carriageway and up into the heart of Michelle Smith's village.

When the chairman of the local community council said: 'Arise Rathcoole and take your place among the nations of the world,' Michelle Smith knew just how much she had achieved.

Michelle remembers: 'I will never forget Rathcoole that evening. There were people lining the streets all the way up along the dual carriageway. By the time we got to the village, it was packed with literally thousands of people there. That was unbelievable. I could not get over how many had come out to welcome me home. I had a fair idea about how excited the village had become during the games, but nothing could have prepared me for this welcome.

'I had heard about The Poitin Still getting huge mileage during the Olympics with camera crews there every night for my races. It is my family's local and my parents are down there often, and The Poitin Still paid for them to go out to Atlanta. My sisters had been the life and soul of the party on the early nights there until Aer Lingus flew them out for the last two finals. It was as if the whole village wanted to share in the delight of the medals – and I was so stunned to discover just how much it meant to my own people on my return. Even now there are people calling on my mother just to see the house where I was born.'

That's typical of the enthusiasm that Michelle Smith still brings to Irish life after her three gold medals in Atlanta. Michelle comments: 'Long may it last! I am delighted to be stopped in the streets in Dublin or Celbridge or anywhere else and asked for my autograph. I am delighted to be recognised as Michelle Smith, the gold medal winner. Signing your autograph when you're a gold medal winner is a lot more exciting that being asked to sign it when you're Michelle Smith the NO-medal loser. I won't ever lose sight of that.

'I suppose the excitement has all but died down, but we're still enjoying it. All of us. My sisters enjoyed all the hype and the craic, but they know when its over, I'm still their sister. My brother, Brian, said that at one stage all the boys in his class wanted to sit beside him after he had been on television.'

In the days after the homecoming, a funny story emerged in the Irish media. The American film agent, Ronnie Leif, claimed Michelle Smith had turned her back on a fortune, that she had rejected an offer from his organisation to make a movie portraying her life and her Olympic dream. There was talk that Michelle had spoken to Tom Cruise and Nicole Kidman about their roles as Erik and the great swimmer. There was talk of Tom Hanks cast as Michelle's father – even though Brian Smith rejected Hanks as being too old. It all got out of hand when the suggested screenplay writer, the author, Gordon Thomas, went public on the claims on the Gerry Ryan radio show.

Michelle and her manager, Kathy Stapleton, had to defend themselves. 'When we were in Atlanta, we were approached by one of the Irish commentators whose neighbour was Gordon Thomas. Gordon's agent in America is a man called Ronnie Leif, a big Hollywood agent who was apparently interested in making a film. It was put to us that this was an opportunity we could not turn down; so we said, "Right; there's no harm in listening."

'It was not the sort of thing where you sit around and wait for it to happen. Kathy and I spoke to Ronnie Leif on the phone, and he said he would come over to meet us before we flew back to Ireland. We met him in Atlanta for dinner and Kathy thought it was a bit funny that he had flown in with no hotel booked, no car and no idea of where he was – even where he was going to go for dinner.

'I wasn't all that bothered on that front. All I wanted to do was to sit down over dinner and hear what he had to say for himself. He started by talking about doing a film that was going to make me one million dollars. In the course of dinner it went up to five million dollars. By the time the coffee had arrived, it was up to ten million dollars. He was talking about a book, a movie and videos – the whole lot across the multimedia spectrum.

'Eventually Kathy asked for some information about his own history. He told us the name of his company and related that he had loads of clients, but he couldn't seem to come up with their names. After two hours, Kathy drove Erik and me back to the village and then she drove Ronnie Leif and his wife back to a hotel. He was to claim later that we had been rude to him and had walked out on him, but that was nonsense.

'Erik was wary of the whole situation from the beginning. The guy wanted permission to act on our behalf in Hollywood. He wanted the go-ahead to organise a book and CD-ROM deals. We were sceptical, so we did not agree to anything he asked. We told him to make contact with our solicitors and then to take it from there. When it was apparent that we weren't going to do business, Ronnie Leif refused to answer some of the fundamental questions we had asked him. We never heard another word from him or about him until all that talk about it on the radio.

'In the end, I saw the funny side of it. According to some of the papers, I was having coffee with Tom Cruise and telling him he wasn't good enough to play Erik in the film! And I was supposed to be worried that Nicole Kidman was too tall to play my role.

'It was all a lot of nonsense. And anyway, if a movie was to be made, it's more likely to be made in Ireland. I'd be more interested in that sort of arrangement.'

One other story was blown out of all proportion on Michelle

Smith's homecoming. Media analysts tripped over themselves to ascertain just how much money she might earn on the back of her three gold medals and the bronze, even though that was almost a sideshow at this stage. Michelle's feelings on the subject are clear. 'On the issue of fees, I feel that having achieved what I have after so many years of hard work, I am now open to offers from any sponsor who wants to do business with me. It is like any other business. When Jack Charlton was manager of the Irish soccer team and charged for appearances, it was fine with everyone. Here, every time I go to an event, someone makes a story out of how much I charged; most of the time their estimates are so far over the top they're laughable.

'When my manager, Kathy, quotes for a job, we are fully aware that we are Irish and that we are looking at an Irish market. Kathy worked in advertising for years, so she is well aware of budgets and what people can and cannot afford. She is not going to ask people for an outrageous amount of money if that is out of line and they cannot afford it. It lends itself to ridiculous situations like the media inquiring if I was charging to go out to meet the paralympic team when they came home from the games in Atlanta. I would never dream of charging for an event like that. It was a pleasure and a privilege to meet Bridie Lynch and the rest of the team and to welcome them home after their great Olympic feat.

'If businesses have money and they can afford to pay me then I will charge them an appropriate amount. If I am asked to do something to help people then I will. It is all relative. There are business areas open to me that I will consider. I am looking into offers to do motivational speeches for corporate businesses both in Ireland and in the States.

'I make no bones about making money from my achievements now. The last four years have not been easy financially on both of us. The most I earned out of swimming before I was 25 was £160 in a competition in Edinburgh in 1994. That money went to my federation and I claimed it in receipts.

'Swimming is much more amateur than athletics. There are probably a handful of swimmers in the world who will make good money. Swimmers do what they do because they enjoy it, not because they want to be rich.

'In January 1995 I secured my sponsorship with TNT and I will always be grateful to them for that support. My biggest Cospoir grant was £7,500. I am not somebody who is motivated by money; I won't turn down money for appearances, but I am not swimming in order to make myself rich.

'And I don't think that, if I make money, it will change me – or Erik. We are not that sort of people. Our goals in life outside the pool are simple. Erik and I would like to have our own home. That would be a nice dream for us. I don't want six cars and millions in the bank. I just want to be happy and content in life, like anyone else.'

CHAPTER THIRTEEN

Drugs

Bad losers will always look for excuses. Bad losers will always try to point the finger, to make accusations, to repeat rumours. In Michelle Smith's case, it seemed as if half a nation auditioned for the role of the bad loser, a role that was to be the only souvenir draped around Janet Evans's neck at the end of the Atlanta games.

There were those at home too who were prepared to spread the rumour of innuendo, overnight experts with no experience of her life in or out of the pool. People prepared to throw stones at the swimmer's house, people who had swum against the bandwagon in the days after Michelle Smith's gold medal Olympics, in the days and nights of her homecoming.

Michelle says, 'I knew going to America that their press would round on me if I won, especially if I was to beat Wagner or Evans in the process. And even at home, there were bound to be people who would go against the common view, people who would write articles for their sensational value. I don't think most of them knew one lane of a 50-metre pool from another lane, but all of a sudden they were all experts on swimming and privy to "inside information" about my life, my coaching, and my preparation – which is impossible because nobody in Ireland knows how I train.'

Michelle Smith also knew going to America that someone, somewhere in summer '96 would drag up the old chestnut of drug abuse in sport. She knew that someone would ask her about her elevation to world-class standard; she knew that some doubting Thomas would question her husband's case history and seek her comments on his disputed ban from international athletics.

Erik de Bruin, a world-class discus thrower and shot-putter, and a World Championship medallist for Holland, is banned from competitive athletics until August 1997, after a famous case that made history and controversy in Dutch sport in equal measure. His story goes back to 1993, a year after he had met Michelle Smith at the Barcelona Olympics.

Erik comments: 'Michelle came with me when I went to an international competition pre-World Championships under the auspices of the IAAF, in Cologne in August 1993, and I was asked to take a random dope test. I had no problem with that and did everything that was asked of me. A few weeks later, I got a call to say that my dope test was positive. The result said that my testosterone level was 6.7 and my HCG level was up as well. Under International Olympic Council rules, levels one to six are okay, six to ten should be investigated, and more than ten means it's clear that something illegal has happened. The IAAF have their own rules; they do not comform to IOC standards. So the international federation asked the Dutch federation to withdraw me from the 1993 World Championships in Stuttgart. My federation in turn asked me if I would withdraw myself.

'I refused. I had done nothing wrong, and I believed that the dope test was incorrect. The Dutch federation came under pressure from the IAAF, which withdrew me from the World Championships as a result. There was nothing I could do about it prior to the World Championships.

'Afterwards, I took my federation to court and the Dutch legal system ruled in my favour. The courts gave me back my right to compete and ruled that the federation had been wrong in their actions. We also proved that the HCG test had been faulty, that it had been carried out on equipment that was not up to standard, equipment that was no longer acceptable in America because of doubts about its accuracy.

'The IAAF parameters are that a level of testosterone above one is considered to be a positive case, so it has got to be a ratio of 1:1 in order to be clear. Mine was 1:6.7. If you compare it to Diane Modhal's, who had a ratio of 1:44 and has since been cleared to compete again, it puts the whole thing into perspective.'

Erik de Bruin had to fight his corner. He had to clear his name. According to the rules of the IAAF, the Dutch federation had to put the case before an independent arbitration.

Erik says, 'When I brought my case to that panel, they came to the conclusion that I should not have been suspended, and they also decided that I should not have got a ban on the results of that test; so my Federation had to accept that. But then the International federation said that they didn't care what this independent panel had ruled. They said they wanted their own arbitration panel to look at the case again. That dragged on for months and months, and finally they held a meeting in Monaco. In short, they said that the IAAF does not make mistakes; so they gave me a four-year ban and refused to recognise the ruling that had been made in Holland by the independent arbitrators. They didn't accept the court ruling that had given me back my right to compete or the independent ruling of the arbitration committee in Holland which had ruled the ban illegal.

'The guy who did the test in Germany simply said, "I don't make mistakes." My lawyer argued the case for human fallibility, but he just insisted, "I don't make mistakes." That was that. I was able to bring my own experts to the arbitration panel in Holland and they told my side of the story, but I couldn't afford to bring all of them to Monaco. I could hardly afford to pay for myself and my lawyer to be there.

'The IAAF had two other experts there arguing their story, but I didn't have anyone to challenge it. You could not describe it like a court room because it wasn't very professionally run. There were no notes taken of what was being said; they tried to record things, but the tape recorder wouldn't work. So in the end, I got a ban for four years until August 1997 which I cannot appeal against.'

Erik de Bruin has lived with the scars of that ban ever since the IAAF upheld their original decision. Now his wife is living with it. He says, 'It haunts you everywhere you go. People hear about the ban and assume you are guilty. At that time, I was ranked second in the world. I was the only athlete that year to beat the world number one, I was second in the World Championships in 1991, and in 1990 I was second in the European Championships. I was at the top of my sport until they banned me. That still hurts; it still annoys me.

'They claimed that I had used illegal substances like testosterone, which is more like a hormone than a steroid. It is a naturally occurring substance in the body and is present at all times. All the test did was to find that mine was slightly higher than normal – but only according to IAAF rules. According to IOC rules it was fine. If I had been tested for the Olympics, nothing would have happened to me. Normal male testosterone goes up and down in cycles. People with certain illnesses can have higher levels than others. My level was not high. I had done nothing wrong; yet I am banned until next year.

'I was aware that it would cause a problem for Michelle in Atlanta and had forewarned her. If you were to ask my views on the use of such substances, I would say that I believe that the same rules should apply to all competing athletes, and that there should always be a level playing field.'

Michelle and Erik have learnt to live with his ban. They knew going to America that it would present problems. They have become accustomed to the questioning – and the testing. Michelle Smith has said many times that she must be the most tested swimmer in the history of her sport.

All those tests have been negative. The questions and the tests haven't stopped though. Up to now, Michelle has not talked about Erik's ban. 'America was the first time Erik's ban was linked to my swimming and that, I have to say, was expected before we went there. In Vienna, after three medals and three press conferences, there was never any reference to those events surrounding Erik and the ban.

'Even though I had a lot of anger built up inside me I maintained my silence on Erik's case. I did not want to discuss it in public after any of the Olympic events. I did not want to make an issue of it.

'I could have done, quite easily. I had lived through the trauma of Erik's trials and tribulations and knew about the hurt he had experienced. I was with him in the stadium on the night of the competition. I went with him to doping control; I was as astounded as he was when the phone call came weeks later. Our reaction was one of total shock, dismay and disbelief. We knew Erik had done no wrong, yet he was being cast under suspicion.

'It's the worst thing that can happen to an athlete. The moment it becomes public knowledge that you have tested positive, your reputation goes on the line. You can lose the support of your public, your sponsors – and your federation. It's only your real friends and family who will stick by you. Thankfully, Asics, his personal sponsors, stuck with Erik. But we knew immediately that there would be a stigma attached. Even when you explain, even when you clear your name, there is always going to be doubt in people's minds.

'The one thing that I liked about Erik's reaction – and the thing that stood out about him — is that from the moment he heard the news and knew that the results weren't right, he said that he would make every effort to clear his name for his own sake and his family's. It would have been easy to bow out of public life, to forget all about his case, and to let everyone forget who he was. That would have been the coward's option — to run away. Erik did not run away. Instead, he fought his corner. Even though they suspended him until the result of the 'B' test, he went to Stuttgart for the World Championships, he held open press conferences and sat there available to public examination in front of the media.

'He told them to go ahead and ask any question they wanted to. He answered them all. By sitting there, by being very open with the facts, the Dutch people were able to get a proper picture of the whole situation. To this day, I believe that the majority of people in Holland will sympathise with Erik. I believe that the majority of people will feel that he has been hard done by. He still has a lot of friends — including people in the media — who helped him, and who want his name cleared.

'He got a ban for something he shouldn't have been banned for. That ban will be lifted next year, but not the heartache. That can never be lifted. Our world fell down around us. The easiest thing would have been to run away from it. Erik didn't. He stood up to the injustice that had been done to him. Even in America, he did not hide the past.'

Ask Erik about the ban now and the pain of that time is still engraved on his heart. It hurts even now to talk about the damage that was done by a German official called Manfred Donike. Ironically, he was to die of a heart attack on board an aeroplane on the very day that Michelle Smith won her first gold medal at the European Championships in Vienna last year.

When Erik was told the news 24 hours later, he said it gave him double reason to celebrate. Callous as it sounded, he meant it; he still means it. 'Manfred Donike had claimed that he was infallible. I know he made a mistake but he was never man enough to admit it. The authorities were afraid to admit it. They knew that if they had admitted that their system was faulty, then half the athletes banned as a result of doping tests would have sued the IAAF for an absolute fortune. It has been said to me that one prominent athletics official was of the opinion that it was better to snare one innocent athlete than to risk lawsuits from another 50 at the time that I was appealing my case.

'I can well believe that attitude. I can also believe some people's theory that it was all a German conspiracy. The three athletes who were capable of beating the German thrower at the '93 World Championships in Stuttgart were all tested in Germany prior to the finals – and all banned for one reason or another.

'Sure, my ban is going to be lifted next year, but that will not right the wrong they did to me. Time hasn't eased the pain. It never will.'

Michelle empathised. 'Like Erik, I am still hurt by the whole thing. There is still a lot of anger over the way in which the whole incident happened and how it was handled. I feel angry because Erik's career was taken away from him at a time when he was coming into his prime. They can never give that back to him, even if they were to admit that they were wrong.'

The Americans had a field day with the Erik de Bruin case after the Atlanta Olympics. They tried to point the finger at Michelle. Every time they asked her if she had ever used performance-enhancing drugs she replied, quite categorically, 'No.' The authorities had the evidence to back up those claims from the swimmer, who believes that she can claim to have been tested more times than any other swimmer in the history of the sport.

Michelle says, 'What annoys me in swimming is that there is a ruling that says that if you are in the top 20 in the world rankings – and prior to the Olympics it was the top 50 – then you have to fill out forms giving your address, telephone number and where you can be contacted within the next 24 hours for doping tests. Then they can arrive at your doorstep at any time, wherever you are in the world. Whenever I leave Holland for more than a day I have to fax my association in Ireland with these forms letting them know where I am going and staying in case they are going to come after me for a dope test.

'That's fine if it's applied to everyone. But it isn't. On the few occasions that they have come to our house in Holland, I have asked them about going into China for testing. They are not permitted in; they have to request that they be allowed in, and then they are only allowed in when the swimmers are on training camp. So the Chinese athletes will know two or three weeks in advance that they are coming. Then it is not a surprise test anymore. I don't object to doing the tests myself as I have nothing to hide. But I do think it is unfair that they can arrive on my doorstep at 9.15 a.m. on a Sunday when I am in my pyjamas, but they cannot do the same thing to the swimmers in China.

'I don't believe that the authorities picked on me because of Erik.' But she has been tested many times. 'I have been tested in my nightdress at home in Holland. I have been tested at the RTE studios in Dublin, after an appearance on the *Gay Byrne Show*, when I came off the air and found the Olympic Council of Ireland doctor waiting for me.

'At the Olympics, the Americans made an issue of the results from the doping tests after my first gold medal. The policy is that results from doping control are never released unless there is something wrong. In America it was released that the doping results from the first day were negative. The clear insinuation was that they were looking for something in the results, but all they got was confirmation that I was clean.' That 13-word statement from the Olympics committee spokeswoman, Michelle Verdier, said simply: 'There is nothing to publicise because there were no results to concern us.' Sadly, that was not enough for the American media.

Janet Evans had fuelled American curiosity with her remarks on the day her star had waned in the Atlanta pool and eight swimmers, not just Michelle Smith, had consigned her to the history books and the 'B' final. She had set in motion a witchhunt that was to see Irish journalists categorically turning on their American counterparts in defence of their heroine. It was a witchhunt that was eventually to see President Bill Clinton apologising for the behaviour of his press corps when he said that he too had had to put up with the 'crap' of the written press.

The American press corps dug deep for their dirt – but failed to find any. They asked coaches, opponents, neighbours, friends, and even foes for anything to hang on the golden girl from Ireland. They failed as miserably as Janet Evans had failed in the pool. They were comprehensive in their search though – even if the answers they got didn't match their incriminating questions.

Their examinations can never take from the achievement even if the hue and cry tainted the gold medal haul of Michelle Smith on her wonderful trek around the Georgia Tech Aquatic Centre. On the night of her second gold medal win, Michelle Smith did exactly what was expected of the new Olympic gold medallist in the 400-metre freestyle. She stood proudly on the presentation podium; she attended the post-race press conference and she presented herself, with Erik by her side, for the post-race drugs test at the doping control centre.

That was also the night that Michelle Smith and the seven other finalists in the 400-metre freestyle condemned Janet Evans to the ranks of swimmers past; simply because she was not good enough; because from her programme it looked as if she had not prepared properly for an Olympics; because she was no longer the queen of middle-distance swimming; because she was slowing with age, and those eight other swimmers were faster. But Evans did not take kindly to the passing of time, and America did not take kindly to the passing of her mantle.

America and American sport, whether it likes it or not, tried to tarnish the image of an Irish golden girl on an Olympic podium. Thankfully, it did not succeed.

CHAPTER FOURTEEN

Sydney

No sooner had the dust settled in Atlanta than preparations began in earnest for the next celebration of Olympic sport. Australia watched. Australia listened. Australia learned as Atlanta struggled to cope with the heat, the humidity, the traffic and the crowds. Atlanta had seen glory; but Atlanta had also struggled with agony, defeat and deceit.

Sydney 2000, the Australians promise us, will be none of the above. It will be organised. It will be majestic. It will be a fitting home for the Olympics as it enters its third century.

Michelle Smith will be 30 by the time Sydney welcomes the world to its southern hemisphere splendour in the year 2000. She will be older and wiser. She will have been four years a champion at three disciplines. Will she be there to defend those three titles? Will she have the same hunger, the same discipline, the same desire that fuelled that gold medal quest in the Atlanta pool? Only time will tell.

For now, it has been fun to enjoy the life of an Olympic champion. She has enjoyed the time that she and Erik have spent in Ireland, luxuriating in the fruits of their Atlanta labours.

She has addressed heads of states, heads of governments, heads of industry, heads of sport. She has been interviewed for school magazines by kids in her temporary domicile of Celbridge, and for worldwide satellite by the cameras of global American media. She has appeared on everything from *A Question of Sport* to the nine o'clock news. She has made television ads for Pantene shampoo, dined with Walter Cronkite at the Celtic Ball in New York and had her photo taken with Liam Neeson at the premiere of *Michael Collins*.

She has been serenaded in song and rhyme, she has had the Beatles

179

hit, which many have mistakenly believed she was named after, recorded in her honour by the Dublin band, The Heartbeats, with the French chorus re-done in her native Irish. The song, on compact disc, has been released as a fundraiser in aid of the Irish Guide Dogs Association. They, in turn, have named one of their newest Labrador puppies 'Michelle' in honour of their new patron.

The golden girl has eaten food from McDonalds in the back of a Rolls-Royce at the bottom of Grafton Street. She has presented prizes to Olympic chefs, opened swimming pools in Ennis, launched kids into a new sport, presented a major horse-racing prize to no less a man than the Aga Khan at Leopardstown racecourse.

And Michelle Smith has hijacked a car. Not quite in the criminal sense though. That little incident came on the day Michelle Smith had to be in two places at almost the same time. In the morning, she was to open the refurbished swimming facilities in Ennis, Co. Clare. That afternoon, she was to present the Irish Stakes Cup to the winner of the big race at Leopardstown. A helicopter had been commissioned to ferry Michelle and Erik first to Clare, and then to the south County Dublin racecourse. But *en route* to Clare, the weather took a turn for the worst. The pilot decided to land, in the middle of a field, in the middle of Co. Clare.

Help was needed to make the launch on time, to keep the appointment, to avoid breaking little hearts. And help arrived. Michelle recalls: 'When the fog began to come in over Clare, the pilot decided that it was too dangerous to go on. He landed in a field, and in the process frightened the life out of all the sheep and the man who owned the land. When we got out of the field, we had to find out where we were. This driver we stopped said he'd drive us to Ennis. He had a car full of kids, but that didn't matter. He literally threw all his family out of the car and onto the side of the road, and took us to Ennis.'

That story is typical of the impact Michelle Smith made with her gold medal pursuit in Atlanta. Now all Ireland wants to know when Michelle Smith will swim again. When will she enter the pool for her first race as a four-time Olympic medallist?

She says, 'Officially, next on the competitive agenda in my swimming career is the European Championships in Seville, one of the most beautiful cities in Spain, next summer. I will do some training work before Christmas, but not at full throttle for six hours a day. Then I will get seriously back into the pool in January and see where we are going. I will also continue to work away from the pool. It would be silly not to.'

Erik continues: 'There are so many things happening for us now; it would be wrong to turn back on the opportunities we have at the moment. We have worked really hard the past two years and in the back of our minds we do want to go to Sydney. However, to go on for another four years with the same level of commitment is going to be very hard for Michelle to maintain. I think we might even decide to do everything low key for the next 20 months, and then get back into the heavy schedule for the two years before the Sydney games.'

Michelle Smith knows she will be 30 come Australia. It is not something that she is worried about, not something she is afraid of. 'Yes, I will be 30 years old for the Olympics in Sydney. But so what? What's the big deal? Ten years ago, there were no swimmers competing at that age; but now there are. Angel Martino from the States is 29 and won a couple of medals in Atlanta. She won a silver in an individual event and was also placed in the relays with the American team. The 1992 Olympic 400-metre freestyle champion, Dagmar Hase, is the same age as I am. There is an Italian breast-stroker who is 33; she would be the oldest. There are a lot of people aged between 26 and 29 in swimming; it is not impossible to compete and win at that stage of your life. I believe my age is one of my strengths. With age has come a new belief and determination.

'My training programme can only be tackled by a senior swimmer. It is only feasible if you have a few years of hard work behind you. You wouldn't give the programme to a 12-year-old. There has to be a base first – years of work and effort before the body is ready to step up to the next level. I believe I can stay at that level for Sydney: certainly not in the four events as I did in Atlanta, but in one or two events. That's a different matter altogether.

'I'm sure some people out there would love me to retire now and to tell them the secrets of our success. Well, I'm only sorry to disappoint them. My training secrets will stay with us probably until I retire. Then I predict they will all be training the way we are now. We could well bring out a video guide called *Winning Gold in the Olympics* right now and do very well out of it – but I don't think we will at the moment!'

Erik comments: 'The training must suit the individual. Michelle's programme suits her. Maybe, with some adjustments, you can make it work for others; but if you copy what she is doing, you won't do a good job. It has to be tailored to the individual.'

Those sorts of opinions do not always sit well with the authorities. In Ireland, swimming is controlled by the Irish Amateur Swimming Association, a body that has not always seen eye to eye with its most successful member.

Michelle says: 'The relationship between the IASA and me has been tetchy ever since they refused to back me financially for my training programme in 1995. They turned me down for finance basically because I was a full-time swimmer in my own right, who wanted to look after my career on my own terms. I had a coach in Erik who was dedicated to my career; a coach who worked with me, and for me and me alone. I was not prepared to work with another coach. For the build-up to the World Championships in 1994, I had done my own thing. For the build-up to the Europeans in 1995 and the Olympics in 1996, I had my own plans, and that was that as far as I was concerned. I was not going to change. I communicated those plans to the Director of Swimming, David McCullough, and we came to a mutual agreement that I was to go ahead with my own programme. They had their own plan for the year 1995. They said, "If you take part in our plan, we'll fund it. If you want to do your own thing, then you're on your own."

'They knew my plans for the World Cup were different from theirs. I wanted to win it. I wanted to achieve something. I wanted to compete and win the World Cup. That meant I had to go to Hong Kong for the first series of races in January 1995, which entailed a big financial outlay. It was an outlay I could not afford at a time when my only sponsorship cheque was for £7,000 from Cospoir. Erik had some support from his personal sponsors, Asics; but it was nothing like the sort of money we needed to fund my bid for real success swimming, for the chance to compete at world level. That meant going to Hong Kong. That necessitated funding from the IASA. We just couldn't afford to pay for the two of us to go over. They had refused to support my plans, so I went to Hong Kong on my own. Erik was my coach for the year and I came home from the Europeans with two gold medals and a silver.'

Nor are things healthy between Michelle and King's Hospital, the club that acted as home to her in her formative swimming years. The club just off the main Galway-Dublin road made the same mistake as the IASA. They tried to impose their way on a swimmer with a will of steel, qualities just as important as that heart of gold in the quest for Olympic honour. The committee and the coaches at the King's Hospital took on Michelle Smith. And they lost.

According to Michelle, 'The relationship with King's Hospital had collapsed a year earlier, at the beginning of 1994. The club didn't like the idea of me doing my own training schedule in their pool. I knew what I had to do to improve, what I had to do to achieve world-class standard. I could already see the improvement that training with Erik and implementing his ideas about marrying my sport with training techniques for track and field had brought about. I wanted to continue with that in the build-up to the World Championships in Rome.

'Training in lanes with the club was not part of that plan. King's Hospital didn't agree. They wanted me to train as part of the club squad. I wanted to do my own thing. They tried to compromise without success. The option they gave me was to do some of my training with the club and the rest of it with Erik. That meant splitting me between two coaches, which was never going to work. I had devised my schedule with Erik, and I wanted to stick with it.

'I sat down with the King's Hospital coach, Derry O'Rourke, and I told him it wasn't going to work. He had been national coach, and he had been Olympic coach. He must have known that there was no way I could split my training between his methods and Erik's. You can't do half of one coach's programme and half of another coach's programme. It simply won't work.

'To be fair to Derry, he agreed with me; but the decision wasn't his. It had been taken above his head in a committee room. They decided that I could either accept their compromise or forget about the arrangement I had had to train with them at my own club, the club I had been so proud of for 13 years previously. I couldn't accept their terms. I had to go my own way, a decision that precipitated our move to Holland. We had no other choice.'

Now Sydney looms large on the horizon. Will Michelle Smith put the nation through another week-long emotional roller-coaster ride? Will she go for gold in four events?

Michelle answers: 'I don't think I'll do four events again – not at the European Championships next summer; not at the World

Championships the following year: and certainly not in Sydney at the turn of the century. The effort would be too intense a second time around. I am very conscious of just how much went into our preparations for the Atlanta games, both mentally and physically. I am not prepared to go for a medal in any distance without that preparation.

'I won't go to any major championship unless I think I'm 100 per cent fit, unless I think I am going there to win. If I'm only 80 per cent ready, I won't go. I was the best in the world in Atlanta, but that doesn't mean I'll be the best in the world come Sydney – at least not without a lot of hard work and dedication. Somebody else can improve over the coming years. As I've always said, an Olympic games can throw up a new name, a new face, an overnight sensation.'

There has been much talk of a suitable national honour in acknowledgement of the achievement Michelle Smith let Ireland share at the Atlanta games. There has been talk of the freedom of her native city, of presidential honours from Mary Robinson, and state honours from Taoiseach John Bruton, leader of the Irish government.

And there has been talk of one thing more than of any other since Michelle Smith kept half the country up half the night in the summer of 1996. It is talk of a 50-metre swimming pool – in a country that has never seen one. It is talk of the Michelle Smith pool.

Michelle says, 'The first thing I want to contribute to this debate is my sincere belief that we do need a 50-metre pool. If you want to train for a major championship, then you have to have access to a 50-metre pool for the last couple of months before your taper. We need the basic facility here.

'On the other hand I don't think it should be used as an excuse when swimmers are not as successful abroad as they might be. World-class swimmers do not spend their lives training in 50-metre pools. They work the short courses, over 25 metres in Europe or 25 yards in America, and then they move up to the 50-metre pool before the major championships.

'There are plenty of 25-metre pools in Ireland where our swimmers can do that preparatory work before they move up to the competition-sized pools. Yet, if you look at how many swimmers we have in the top ten world rankings over 25 metres, I think it may only be two. If we were to automatically have a world champion or an Olympic champion as soon as we developed a 50-metre pool, then why don't we have the same thing at the 25-metre level where there are plenty of pools available?'

Erik continued: 'I think Irish swimming and Irish swimmers have to look in the mirror. Too often, when they go abroad, they are happy just to compete against the big names of world swimming. I have seen too many events where some of the Irish entrants just stop short of asking the big names to sign autographs.

'There is also a tendency to use the lack of a 50-metre pool as the big excuse. But while it is needed, it will not produce world records or world champions overnight. The attitude has to change – not just the size of the pool.

'To suggest that I am the man to change that is nonsense. Erik de Bruin as the national coach will never happen. I don't fit in with the structure of the Irish swimming federation, I can't work within their structure, their ways. I have already done some work with other swimmers, and I believe that I will do so again. But it will not be with the IASA. I can only work with athletes who are willing to put out a lot of work, as much work as Michelle has put in over the past four years.

'There are too many athletes out there who annoy me, who talk about doing the work but aren't prepared to carry it through, and then they wonder why they don't succeed. So far, all I have done is help coaches and swimmers with advice on coaching. I will continue to do that, but not as an Irish national coach.

'It is a sad thing to say, but I seriously think that swimming in Ireland is doomed to fail as long as the IASA have the kind of organisation that they have at the moment. Swimming is for the officials: they are not helping the swimmers to achieve their goals or to get to a higher level. In too many cases than there are for my liking, it is my opinion that some of them are there because they like positions of power. Their rules and codes of conduct are more important than how well the swimmers are doing; they are more important than what's good for the swimmers.

'We did not know how much they were trying to take some of the glory for Michelle's achievements because we were removed from this situation in Atlanta. They tried last year to make a presentation at the TNT reception after the European Championships but Michelle gave it back.'

Michelle continued. 'The point was that they asked me if I wanted a presentation made to me on their behalf. I wrote back saying that I didn't want to have one made but they still tried to make it at another reception without telling anybody. It wasn't on, as I had already told them twice that I didn't want a presentation. It didn't help our relationship. However, I do have regular contact with David McCullough, the Director of Swimming. He is trying to do the best he can in his own way, but I think his powers are quite limited as well.'

So what is the desired legacy of three gold medals and a bronze for Ireland in the pool at the Atlanta games?

Michelle said, 'Erik and I would dearly love to see an improvement in facilities for all Irish swimmers, not just for those who will benefit from the provision of a 50-metre pool. I'd love to see the motto, "sport for all", becoming a reality.'

And Erik went on. 'It can be done. It would be good for Irish swimming for example if they made it easier for clubs to get access to pool time. In some cases, they have to pay £50 an hour for the use of the pool at 6 a.m. just to get their swimmers into the pool. That is an exorbitant amount of money to charge for the use of a pool at that time of day since there is no demand for it then. Clubs with 200 members or less can't afford that. So they don't have access to as much pool time as they would like. There is no need for pool managers to charge that sort of money at that time of the day. In Germany clubs are not charged for pool time. The facilities should be there for the public. That makes it easier for clubs to invest more in coaching and competition, investments that will benefit the club and their swimmers in the long run. Otherwise they would have to put so much money into the rental of the pool that there would be nothing left for all the other areas.'

Michelle was equally realistic. 'That also takes away from the coaching for so many Irish clubs. Because they have to spend so much money on pool hire, they don't have money to pay coaches a good salary or to send them away to competitions, seminars, or tuition courses abroad. The coaches suffer as well. Sometimes the coaches get disheartened. They do so much without the support that is vital to their jobs. A lot of them don't get paid for it or, if they do, it's not a lot. They coach because they enjoy it, and because they are dedicated to their sport and their swimmers.'

And no, there won't be a generation of water babies born on the back of one Olympic triumph. Certainly, Michelle says, 'I don't see a whole generation of Michelle Smiths coming up overnight. There will have to be a lot of changes made to the structure of the swimming association, the club structure, and basic facilities available. In Holland, I have a number of pools on my doorstep. In Ireland, a young kid who wants to swim may have no pool within striking distance. The infrastructure is not there.'

Erik concluded: 'There are plenty of 25-metre pools in Ireland. It's just that sometimes they are not as well maintained as they should be. Perhaps the government should look at upgrading those facilities and making them available to more people.'

In international terms, the European Championships in August 1997 is the next major date on the swimming calendar, on Michelle Smith's calendar. Will she be there, standing on the block for the first time as an Olympic champion? Standing there just as Evans, Egerszeggi and Hase have all done in the past? Standing there to be shot down? Standing there to be beaten? Or will she be standing their to win, to win like the great champion she is? How will she feel? But first of all, will she be swimming?

Michelle replies, 'I will take it the same way as I took the first race at the Olympics: I will treat it the same as any other race. When you're standing on the block for the next major international, the person beside you doesn't care if you're an Olympic champion, world champion or European champion. All she wants to do is to beat you.'

Erik says, 'At the moment, we're trying to decide if Michelle wants to go on at full throttle for another four years. It is going to be very difficult to keep mentally fresh for another long spell. I think Michelle may take it very easy for the next year and a half; she may not even go to the Europeans, but just train, train and train with some small competitions along the way. She has to relax mentally for that year before really going for it again. But that is only one of the options. However, if she really wants to be there again over the next four years, it is going to be very hard to keep up that momentum, that dedication, that concentration.'

To win all the major championships would leave Michelle very tired mentally. Does she want to be tired at the end of those four years when the Olympics come around? Michelle and Erik will have to make those decisions. They alone will have to decide when the curtain comes down on this wonderful odyssey, this myriad of emotions.

As Michelle says, 'I don't know how long I will continue as a swimmer. I will take things as they come. When it is no fun anymore, I will quit.'

Erik agrees. 'When you don't like it anymore, there is no point in carrying on. But as long as you enjoy something, as long as you like doing your work, then why should you stop? Some people will say that she will be too old for the next Olympic games. That's rubbish! They told Michelle that years ago after Barcelona and look at her now.'

Michelle is quite emphatic: 'I will quit either when I no longer enjoy swimming or when I feel I cannot improve anymore. I do think that there is still room for improvement in everything. I have only been training like this for the last three and a half years. I have had to learn a different way of training. Erik has had to learn how to coach me. We are still learning. Every year, when we go to a major championship, we see something that we know we can improve on for the next competition.'

But for Erik, the decision has already been made. His IAAF exile from athletics ends in 1997; but his self-imposed exile will never end. 'I will not go back to competing when my ban is up. I have problems with the cartilage in my hips – it is partly gone – and, besides that, I have been out of it for too long. I enjoy coaching; that is my discipline now. You cannot be an athlete and a coach at the same time.

'I would not have believed it in Barcelona if I had been told then that in four years' time I would be a swimming coach; but who knows where or what I will be in another four years.

'I do have ambition. I am interested in a lot of sports, not just track and swimming. When I talk to people who are in sport, I am always interested in how they train. When I first met Michelle, I was always asking her about her training methods. That interest is something I would like to develop. I have said it to Michelle many times that I would be interested in working with horses, in doing the same sort of training with them, to see how thoroughbred racehorses would respond to such training.

'Some of the theories we have adapted for swimming may be possible with horses. I'm just not sure what sort of work I could do with them in a gymnasium. And what sort of response would I get from the rest of the people in the gym?'

Michelle is confident about her husband's abilities. 'I've no doubt Erik can coach anyone – or any horse. When Erik is working with people, whether an athlete or a swimmer, he has a way of relating to the athlete that is unique. Because he has competed at that international level, he can explain to the person where he or she is going wrong and how he or she can improve. He knows what to say at the right time to make the athlete perform. Not every coach has that ability. Some coaches know how to do things correctly, but they cannot relate their ideas to the athlete.

'Erik doesn't just go by coaching manuals; he uses his own initiative and thinks up new methods for us to try out. They have consistently worked. I have never been sceptical about his ability. I have always been open to trying new ways. When he explained his training methods to me, they made sense. The theory is very simple and very straightforward. He has combined the ways of the athletics world with the needs of the swimming world.

'And Erik is the first to say that one of the secrets to my success is a lot of hard work and dedication. I am not necessarily the most talented of the swimmers that competed in the races in Atlanta because I haven't got the perfect build for swimming. But I am one of the hardest working of all swimmers.

'The correct mental approach is also important. It is not just about the most talented, the fittest and the hardest worker. You have to be able to do it on the day, to handle the pressure, to have the will and the determination along the way.'

That will – that determination – takes a lot out of any athlete. How much longer can Michelle Smith carry on?

'There will come a time when I will want to retire. When? I don't know. If I was to want to retire before Sydney, it wouldn't particularly bother me. I have my Olympic medals now; nobody can take them away from me. For Sydney, I may decide to narrow my races down and specialise in one stroke.'

All that is debate for the future. For the present, Michelle Smith is the human face of Irish swimming – even Irish sport. Has it all served to change the girl from Rathcoole who took on the world and won?

Michelle says, 'I don't know if swimming has changed me to any extent, but it has made me in some ways the person that I am. I am now happier than I have ever been, my relationship with Erik has a lot to do with it.

'But I have to be careful not to get drawn into the hype. I have to be the same person that I was beforehand, even though the world is going crazy around me. That's the most important thing. To be true to myself through all of this.'

And what if Brian Smith had never taken the time or the interest to take his little girl swimming?

Michelle is philosophical. 'I'm not one to look back and wonder what would have happened if my father hadn't brought me to the pool and taught me how to swim. There are a lot of things that happen just by chance. If I had never met Erik, if we had never got involved in 1992, I wouldn't be here either. I don't know what would have happened to me if we had never met. I don't know if I would have stayed in Ireland or in Houston. I might even have stayed in Canada. Who knows? There are too many uncertainties in that sort of a debate.'

There is one certainty, though, in Michelle Smith's life right now. The certainty is that she is an Olympic champion three times over. One colour dominates her life, her achievement, her contribution to the world of sport.

It is the colour of gold.

Photo credits

The authors and publishers are grateful to the following for permission to reproduce copyright photographs: Gerry Mooney; Photogenic; RTE Sports Television Ireland; Billy Stickland; Star Newspapers Ireland; Jim Walpole. Every effort has been made to contact copyright owners but in some cases this has not been possible.